MW01138365

The Jingle Factor II

Christmas Spirit To The Letter

By Rita Brumm, R.M.A.

Rita Brumm
4405 South Redbud Avenue
Broken Arrow, OK 74011

rita@adgenieoftulsa.com

ISBN-13:978-1545160824
ISBN-10:1545160821

Table of Contents

Introduction...v

A..1

B..7

C..15

D..29

E..39

F..45

G..61

H..71

I..77

J..83

K..89

L..97

M...103

N...113

O...119

P..125

Q...131

R...133

S..141

T..147

U...151

V..153

W...157

X..167

Y..169

Z..171

About the Author..173

Introduction

Welcome to my second book! Those of you who have my first book, *The Jingle Factor: Twelve Months of Christmas Spirit*, own a 12-month guide to getting---and giving---Christmas "jingle" all year long! And those readers know my inspiration to write both books came from a holiday pin I purchased during Black Friday at my local Stein Mart store two years ago. It is truly amazing how such small things can inspire such large life changes.

The Jingle Factor II: Christmas To The Letter, takes being a "Jing"-ologist to the next level! Now you can discover ways to "jingle-ize" both your life---AND the lives of others---with my complete A-Z guide. Jingle...Alphabet-ized!

Full of even more real-life stories, humor and yes---even a few life observations sprinkled in --- *The Jingle Factor*

II promises to help you laugh and learn your way "By the Letter" to a happier life. From, As Seen on TV to Dating, Queen-ing to Shopping, and everything in between, you'll find all kinds of ways to "jingle" by the LETTER.

So, keep calm and Jingle On! And I hope you have an even MORE "jingle-tastic" life as a result. As in my first book, a percentage of all book sales will benefit the Bartlesville Kiddie Park in Bartlesville, Oklahoma.

The Jingle Factor II
Christmas Spirit to the Letter

A

As Seen on TV

We've all seen these hilarious advertisements (Promise Pitches) as I like to call them. You can't escape them, no matter how much channel surfing you do. From sixty-seconds to sixty-minutes, someone has spent some serious dollars trying to sell you your own personal miracle. But instead of evading them, embrace them for all the jingle they're worth!

From dentures in a day to veggie dicers to adult diapers, the jingle possibilities are endless. From glue that will fuse anything to concoctions that will cure everything, you can jingle yourself silly over the ridiculous claims they make. This is the best show in town. Who needs Netflix?

My favorites:

The one-size-fits-all pillow. (NO pillow fits everyone).

The ear wax remover that looks like an insulin syringe. And comes in COLORS for the whole family! (Top on MY list....NOT.)

The **"glove groomer" for animals that lets you pet and groom your dog at the same time.** (They DO know the difference. And you will most likely be facing an im-PAWS-ible task). Keep band-aids handy; you'll need them.

The blanket with three holes in it they jokingly call a robe. You know what I'm talking about! (Add a hood, and you'll look like a lost Tibetan monk without his GPS. Or worse yet, some type of cult member.....I don't recommend going outside for the morning paper dressed like that. You may not return.)

Strobe Toilet bowl lights. (Yes, being able to see yourself perform bodily functions in the middle of the night is enough to keep you UP all night!)

Wrinkle remover cream. (All this removes is money from your wallet. And the effect rinses off WITH the cream.)

"Welder in a Week" type trade schools who promise short-term classes and tall salaries after graduation. (They just don't say how LONG after graduation.)

"Designer" adult diapers. (only the NAME is designer)

Insomnia cures. (entertaining, but ineffective.)

Prescription drugs, whose SIDE effect list takes up more room on the pill bottle than the ACTUAL effect it's SUPPOSED to have. My favorite: a stop-smoking drug that can help you stop SMOKING, but could START a lot more stuff. Like depression, suicidal tendencies, dry mouth, constipation, diarrhea, heart palpitations and hair loss. So you may stop smoking, but you could wind up feeling and looking like an escapee from Zombie Wars. You might be trading your ONE stop-smoking drug prescription in for LOTS more, like Ex-Lax, Prozac, Valium, Pepto-Bismol and Rogaine. And which is just enough stress on your body ---and your wallet--- that you might start your habit again! Really? Wow. And they get your money a SECOND time! Now THAT'S marketing!

Credit Card Consolidation Companies. (Yes, they may reduce your existing debt, and they don't share that doing this will obliterate your future credit for YEARS.)

Some ideas I have for new inventions?

----**Spray-on Toupees** (self-explanatory)

-----**Mailbox Butler** (Wire to a connection inside that tells you when your mail has arrived.)

-----**Mailbox MP.** Because we have had so many mailbox thefts around my city over the last few months, this handy little alarm sounds as soon as a would-be thief pulls the handle. If they are dumb enough to continue and reach their hand in, a spring set of handcuffs pushes their hand to one side and locks it.

----**Pen Police.** Great for any bank lobby. Try to steal a lobby pen, and it triggers a hand-slapper that shouts: Shame, shame! When my bank told me they lose an average of 1,000 pens a year, this little invention, which only costs $38 to make, would be well worth the time.

----**Press-On Jeans.** It's getting them OFF that may prove to be interesting.

Air Show

Your spirits will soar as high as the planes. I particularly enjoy the events featuring historical aircraft from World

War II. If there's not one in your area, it's worth the trip to find one. If you can ever attend a Blue Angels event, go! We have several in Oklahoma; one of the best is in Muskogee.

Attitude

Remember, a bad attitude is like a flat tire. You can't go anywhere unless you change it. Attitude determines altitude; you can have as much jingle as you THINK you can! Every week, do a Mental Diet; increase your intake of positive thoughts, and eliminate all those negative things from the plate of LIFE. It's guaranteed to reduce your stress and keep your attitude in great shape!

Ships don't sink because of what's AROUND them; it's what gets INSIDE them. So don't let outside drama get inside you and weigh you down. Remember, It's not what's in front of you that blocks you, it's what inside you that holds you back from the jingle you deserve. Think of life's problems like a scuff on the loafer of life. A little polish, and it's all new again.

B

Baby

Holding a precious baby in your arms will put jingle in ANY day. But be sure you are EQUIPPED for the adventure. It's all about ACCESSORIZING. Adorn your "visit-the-baby-day" outfit with an extra-absorbent receiving blanket, leak-proof bottles and industrial strength diapers beforehand. And to all you hoop earring wearers, stick to studs for this day, because a curious baby seeing that swinging, shiny metal ring hanging down from your face may be soon handing you the earring, and part of your EAR right along with it. Doing all of the above will ENSURE that you will not need to make a wardrobe change or a trip to the ER as part of your day!

Back to School Day

If you've got school-age kids, this is major cause for parental jingle. After a long summer of kids at home trashing every room they can find, testing your patience and taking your grocery budget for the month to zero in a week, we are seriously jingle-challenged. We love them; but we also love the day they go back to school. Seriously, in our neighborhood, moms waited just long enough to see the bus vanish from sight before WE vanished from sight, to appear ten minutes later at our neighborhood IHOP to celebrate with caffeine overload and as much sugar as we could ingest. Yes, I was one of them. And we got to share enough summer holiday horror stories that would never be story material for Sesame Street. But the other kids always got into more trouble than my daughter ever did, so I always left feeling grateful for the calmer life I had! When the kids are back in school, the HOUSE is back in order!!

Ballet Up To The Barre

Attend at least one in your lifetime. The incredible symmetry of graceful motion blended with stirring music will give you jingle well beyond the performance. My personal favorites: The Nutcracker, The Sleeping Beauty and Beauty and The Beast.

Band

Whether it's a big band, marching band, bluegrass or jazz band, go hear one! From "In the Mood" to Moody Blues, a live band stirs your soul. The Super Bowl for Bands: The Tournament of Roses parade. Go see it or get it on the tube before the Rose Bowl.

Beach

Life's a beach.....and it doesn't have to be in the Caribbean. It can be a carved out stretch of sand on a picturesque lake, river or pond. Just watching the waves gently rippling on the shore can give you jingle like no other. Don't have one nearby? No problem. Create your own beach address..... INSIDE! Our dear friends Dennis and Sharon furnished their entire condo in what I call "Classic Beach," featuring accents of sea shells, fish sculptures, boats and lighthouses. You're on vacation as soon as you walk in the door and see one of a number of mood-inspiring signs, including "This Way to the Beach; Or (my favorite) "What Happens At the Beach is Laughed At The Rest of the Year."

One thing I love about packing for the beach is that--- in contrast to your swimsuit---your flip flops fit you EVERY year!

But if you can afford to "shell" out the cash and go to the Caribbean.....well, bon voyage!! (And if people need to reach you, just have them call your "shell" phone.)

Boat Ride

So if your answer to the question, "Got Yacht?" is a rowboat, canoe or a party pontoon, it doesn't matter! While you're not on the same TYPE of boat as someone else, you'll experience the same wavelength of jingle in the water!

Books

Enter the world of books, and you can be anyone you want, go anywhere you want, and do anything you want...WITHOUT a passport! (OR TSA taking you to a back room because your set of electric hair rollers looked like 12 sticks of rubber TNT. See TRAVEL) Books transport you to a world of jingle of your own imagination. You can be a wild game hunter in Africa, a world-renowned detective solving mysteries with Sherlock Holmes, a Rock Star, movie star, TV star or any other star you want to be. Anytime you want! Books educate, entertain, encourage and engage like few other things can. With today's technology, you can carry the world on your Kindle.

Bowling

That's right. Anyone of any age with a pulse can enjoy a couple of hours throwing a three-holed ball down a hard-wood floor at ten painted vertical posts. It's also a great way to beat stress. As you know, those "pins" have an amazing resemblance to the human form. So....imagine it; those pins could be your boss, your ex, your in-laws, irritating co-worker, demanding client, or anyone else who tries to steal your jingle. Whether you win or lose is irrelevant. You're throwing something...legally. <u>Spare</u> the time; you'll be glad you did. You will soon be in a great "frame" of mind! (And it's a lot cheaper than therapy).Plus, your life will soon be in the "jingle" lane. Hopefully, with no side trips to the GUTTER!

Bumper Stickers/Car Tags

If I could stay behind the wheel all day, I would, just for all the jingle I get from seeing bumper stickers, or bumper SNICKERS, as I like to call them.

I'm not speeding, I'm qualifying.

Driver only carries $20 in ammunition.

My podcast can beat your blog.

I brake for...nothing.

I brake for...men/women carrying American Express Platinum.

Honk if you love lasagna.

My other car is at college.

Driver carries no cash...he's married.

My other car is...at the auto auction.

Frankly, Scallop, I don't give a Clam. (Maine car tag)

A car tag.

Some bumper stickers I have seen on WOMEN'S cars:

Coffee, Chocolate, Men...Some Things Are Just Better Rich.

If you want breakfast in bed, sleep in the kitchen.

I brake for mood swings.

Warning: I have an attitude and I know how to use it.

So many men, so few who can afford me.

Some tags I just can't mention here, because they reflect that the car owner's combined brain wattage wasn't enough to power a nightlight. And I'm scared to think that these people are even driving a car.

C

Car

Oh, yeah, nothing can give you jingle like the jingle of a new set of car keys in your pocket. Whether it's new or used, a truck, car or SUV, it's new for YOU! And inhaling that new car smell at the dealership can be more intoxicating than a double margarita. It's all yours once you can get past those three little words: "with approved credit."

Since I love Christmas movies, I also wound up seeing one too many Christmas year-end clearance car commercials (especially the one where Santa goes into the North Pole launch chamber, and swaps his "sleigh ride" for a revved up red BMW) and went on a mission to buy my own red ride. But the process of buying your dream ride can take you on quite another type of

ride, and can leave you jingle---as well as wallet---chal-
lenged if you're not careful.

I worked for a year in internet sales at a car dealership.
You wouldn't believe some of the car sale stories I could
share. Like the customer who took literally our "push,
pull or drag in your trade" offer. This car had been
crushed into a twisted 5x5 foot metal ball by some auto
yard after he'd wrecked it, but he SAID it WAS a 2004
Chevrolet Camaro. (Wasn't that enough?) And he
wanted top dollar for it. After all, he had PICTURES.
Plus, the license tag was still showing. Or the woman
who asked our finance manager WHICH tax return he
wanted to process her credit application, the one where
she made money, or the one where she lost money. O-K.
She had both. Yep, both.

My first quest for my "red ride" did not work out well, either. I had test-driven the car I saw online Friday the next
day, which not only was a Saturday, it was the last day of
the year and part of a three-day holiday weekend, which
meant three days without access to my bank (who knew I
was looking). I told the salesman before I ever drove the
car that this was the situation. He had said, "no problem,
if we can come to an agreement on the price, you can
leave with the car today." Well, I drove the car, loved the
car, and the price was right. And I'm sitting there trying
to determine how I was going to leave WITH the car

WITHOUT giving them any money. Maybe it was one of those "you pick it out, we work it out" kind of deals, I thought. He wrote up the contract, and then said, "just give us a check for the car, and we'll just "hold" it for you until you get your financing done next week." WHAT? REALLY? His "no-problem" solution was to have me write a check so full of rubber, it would bounce all the way to Dallas and back. He brought in the finance manager, who said the same thing, and seemed insulted that I would not "trust" them to hold an $18,000 check. Number one, It's illegal, and #2, it's illegal. And then I was told it was "done all the time." I was never offered the option of leaving a deposit, with the remainder to be paid upon delivery of the bank draft for the balance. (That's how it was always done when I grew up.)

I went to my bank the following Tuesday, after I had already had THREE more calls from the salesman. I said I would call after my meeting, which I did; I told him then that I would have to wait until the loan paperwork processed, which would be the next day. Sell the car if you have to, is what I said. After all, it's a CAR, not my dream house in the Hamptons. He said he had a solution--- again--- and would call me back after he spoke with said same finance manager. Two minutes later, the phone rang again, and I quickly realized I was on a speakerphone; and I hear the salesman say, "We'd like to call your bank." I said, "WHAT? And WHY?" "Weeell, we just kind of need to verify all this," he continued. I ended the call....and the deal. I had just verified that I needed to go somewhere ELSE. The new car smell was gone; it was replaced by a very bad TASTE. So my advice is, keep a $20,000 stash of cash under your mattress or a very full bank account at all times so you can buy a car on demand; because that's what they will ask for. I think I "auto" go somewhere else. And did.

Cat

A new feline friend can give you plenty of jingle! The pitter-patter of tiny paws can certainly be the PURR-fect addition to your family. Just be sure to take all the precautions so it doesn't become a "CAT"- astrophe. First, the right litter box. (those ones that automatically circulate, wrap, and redeposit new litter are the best. And watching your cat watch the gadget work is jingle in itself.) Secondly, buy a REALLY BIG scratching post, unless you want your furniture to look like an ad for Battered Homes and Ghettos. Remember, unlike dogs, cats can jump high and get into places they don't belong, so leaving that chicken casserole on top of the counter will frustrate a dog, but furnish a feast for a cat...and all her friends. And forget about bathing them. You will AL-WAYS wear more water than they will. (Plus a few scratches) Cats are wonderful cuddlers and do make great lap pets. My childhood cat Fluffy (yes, that really was her name) loved to jump up on the side of my piano and watch me practice. I figured out in short order that what she REALLY loved was watching for an opportunity to "catch" the METRONOME . Well, it finally caught HER on a downbeat and sent her to the floor. She never came onto the piano---or even the ROOM---again. Too bad, she was a pretty good accompanist.

Change

...the way you look at things, and the things you look at will change. Be open to new experiences; get out of your comfort zone. Change your hairstyle, dump those 80's suits (unless you just like looking like an NFL linebacker) with the huge shoulder pads, pitch the pantyhose (it takes ten minutes to pull them on anyway), get tinted contacts, wear higher heels, take a computer class, try zumba. Wear colored underwear, and buy a car that isn't black or beige just because the insurance is cheaper.

Often, when you take the time to give things and people a second look, you will also decide to give them a second chance. Like the nerdy guy with glasses who you find out OWNS the trendy restaurant you only thought he did the books for. BE the change you want to see in the world. Accept what is, forget what was, and have faith that there will be a happy future. Think of your life as a real-time book you are writing. If you don't like how you've written one of the chapters, rewrite it or even eliminate it to ensure a more jingle-filled outcome. Be the star in your own life.

Christmas

In my first book, *The Jingle Factor: Twelve Months of Christmas Spirit*, I spent a lot of time talking about Christmas. It's the ultimate "jingle-fest" of the year. While the holidays are a time of meetings, greetings and eatings with family and friends, don't forget the reason for the season and get your tinsel in a tangle! Plan ahead, and spend more time with family.Don't risk getting "mall"-ed!" Plan for your "holiday traffic" of family and friends, and you'll jingle all month long. Another way you can have Christmas all YEAR long? Keep your tree up (unless it's real, then buy a cheap one) and just change the ornaments; e.g., Hearts for Valentine's Day, Shamrocks for St. Patrick's Day, painted eggs and bunnies for Easter. One friend of mine celebrated the arrival of football season with a tree covered in baby footballs, foam fingers, and "football food" ornaments of plastic hot dogs, chips and popcorn on strings.

Need more ideas? During the summer months, hang flip flips over your mantel instead of stockings. Put up a string of lighted chili peppers around your patio. Buy extra sheets of Christmas-themed POSTAGE STAMPS and use them ALL YEAR LONG on packages, greeting cards, even on your income tax bill. (Maybe it will jingle them enough you won't get audited) It will keep the recipients jingling. How about holiday MUSIC? I keep at least two Mannheim Steamroller Christmas CDs in my car at all times to play when I need "Christmas on the Go." Even when it's 100 degrees in the shade, I'm feeling cooler just HEARING "White Christmas!"

Santa works year-round on getting ready for Christmas, too. There's always new sleigh guidance software and additional global distribution markets to research.

Computers

Yes, take a BYTE of jingle for your life...right from your COMPUTER!

You can tell those people who are not so computer savvy. When you say the word "modem," they think that's what they're supposed to do to the weeds in their backyard. Knowing your way around a computer can give you lots of jingle, if you just know how to do it! It can be APP-solutely amazing, in fact.

Like the internet. Besides Facebook, the general Internet offers all kinds of ways to find out everything...about anything or anyone. From what Carrie Underwood feeds her dog to how to build your own climate-controlled outhouse, it's a search engine that will help you broaden your own personal track to knowledge and fun.

Even if it's weird. How about "How to Parallel Park in Less Than 20 Minutes Without An Insurance Claim." "How to Bathe Using ONLY Five Soaps and Shampoos." "Brain Surgery For Dummies." "Coffee Breaks on $5 A Day." You can see a doctor about your allergies, learn how to fix that leaky faucet, buy that new mother-of-the-bride dress. So go ahead; go ga-ga over Google. You know you're really getting your jingle on the computer when you go online before you go get your first cup of coffee.

I have a self-confessed computer geek girlfriend who is having husband issues. And this is how she described it to me:

After I upgraded Boyfriend 4.0 to Husband 1.0, the program started changing. It instantly caused limited access to wardrobe, flower and jewelry applications that performed well under Boyfriend 4.0., Husband 1.0 uninstalled other valuable programs, including Dinner-Dancing 4.3, Cruise 2.5, and SymphonyNight 5.2. It replaced these with distinctly inferior programs, including PokerNight 3.1, MondayNightFootball 4.1 and Golf 3.6. Conversation 6.0, ChildCare 3.3 and Laundry 2.7 no longer function, and crash the system every time they are initiated with Husband 1.0. Running Nagging 5.4 to repair Husband 1.0 has not worked to date. (I wonder if her uninstalled programs would reappear if she ran a test program for Separation 3.8?) My mother always told me that the best way to get a man to do something is to just suggest he is too old for it. Works every time.

Cook

Go ahead...BAKE it happen. For your family. For a friend. For your spouse. Because you just want sugar. Or need a "fried fix." It's comforting, and just makes you feel jingle-fied all over. If your recipes turn out more like "mess-ipies," and your home-cooked meals taste more like appetizers with ambition, eat someone else's! It's called "DELIVERY!" I personally love to cook, but my FAVORITE thing for dinner is STILL reservations! And sometimes I just have to tell my family that "your DISH is NOT my command!" (at least not TODAY).

And by the way, if you DO cook, please follow directions. If the recipe says to put the turkey in the sink to chill for a few hours, it does NOT mean to not put a bottle of wine under its wing and hand it the TV remote.

I consider myself a pretty good cook, and I know about timers. However, one of my friends has her own: the smoke alarm. When it goes off, dinner is done.

Another dear friend of mine, a self-admitted, cook-only-under-protest person, once invited us all over for a chili party to celebrate a relative's birthday. She made six pounds of this meal. She figured it was simple, and after all, how could she ruin chili? Well, she found a way! We all filled our bowls, sat down, and realized something VERY quickly...she forgot to add the CHILI POWDER! So we had six pounds of ground meat and tomato sauce.

Of course, we all have those extra busy days. Those are the days when cleaning up the dining room means getting the empty fast food bags out of the back seat of the car.

I once attended a friend's Sunday brunch. I was handed a gray-colored plate that looked like a hubcap with Eggs Benedict on top of it. Wait for it: "Well, there's no place like chrome for the hollandaise!"

Remember, Life is what you bake it!

Count

...your blessings. It may seem trivial, but look in the mirror for at least two minutes every morning and say out loud what you're thankful for, especially on those days where you feel like your blessing meter is registering a -20. Make it a goal to state at least one blessing every morning, and write it down on a board or notebook. If you read my first book, that book is your Jingle Journal. It will all add up to making you feel pretty good about yourself! I like to call it the "blessing booster." It can perk up your day faster than that second cup of coffee. (But never forget the coffee! You need to be able to SEE the mirror!)

Cruise

If you haven't already, take at least one (or a dozen!) in your lifetime. Think of it as a giant floating hotel, with an 24/7 ocean view, which delivers YOU to all kinds of geographic thrills. If I were a travel agent, I'd advertise it this way: "OCEAN VIEW: WHEREVER YOU SLEEP!" Where the view from your stateroom changes with the day, sometimes even the hour! (So don't ever nap too long; you may find that your ship is now in a different country). All you have to do is step off the ship

(DO wait until they dock; the water is VERY deep there, and to those hungry seagulls hovering overhead, you'll look like a giant seafood buffet). You can be gazing at a sandy beach today, and viewing mountain rainforests to-morrow. Cruising is good for your health; haven't you heard of Vitamin Sea?

Between the two of us, my husband and I have been on ten. We liked them so much, we even got MARRIED on one. And that's a story Bob and I---plus a very stressed wedding director--will never forget. On the way out of my house, I bumped my left thumb--with it's newly applied artificial nails I had done the day before---into the wall in the front hallway as I picked up my suitcase. It bled a little, but I dismissed it, as our friends were already at the door to pick me up for the ride to the airport. By the time we boarded the ship, my fingernail was the size of a guitar pick. I said nothing to my fiance, and somehow got through the wedding, pictures and reception. THEN, I said to him, "Take me to the infirmary...NOW." His memorable response was, "What? Sick of me already?" I then showed him my throbbing appendage, and we rushed down there...in full bridal attire.

They had to surgically remove my entire left thumbnail, as by then it was starting to make a home in the finger tissue. Nurses had to wrap my wedding dress more than the finger for the surgery. Doctor Brook said we were definitely the best-dressed people there, plus they had never had a newlywed couple with THIS problem. They wrapped it up, told me to "avoid water" for the week (like that was going to happen on a CRUISE) and sent us away with pain pills (and probably gave THEM-SELVES a huge dose of LAUGHTER AFTER we left.) We were called later in the week by the head nurse sup-posedly to report in for a "wound check," and were promptly presented with a picture of the whole medical team holding up their thumbs, with a sign in front saying "Thumbs up to Bob and Rita for a great life to-gether! The Carnival *Valor* Medical team." Quite a con-versation starter for future dinner parties.

Another fun activity you can see on a cruise...if you're lucky. Stay aboard in one port instead of going ashore, and watch the crew do their lifeboat drills! We were stuck in our stateroom in one port (sunburn), but got our jingle just seeing the best show of the day right from our balcony (think about it; free show with private seating, air conditioning and room service.) If you could see my video, you would see what looked like a dozen little miniature orange submarines wildly buzzing around in circles. They would nearly ram each other, back up, turn, and nearly collide into another group of little orange boats. It was Bumper Boats at sea! Two people nearly fell off their posts. (The only thing that worried me was that if there was a REAL emergency in the open ocean, they would probably sink the rescue craft.)

D

Dance

...on the sidewalk, in the subway, in the street! And do it like no one's watching. Or even if they are! It's an amazing way to get your jingle. But let's face it, folks, there are just some people who are better qualified for "Dancing in the Bars" than "Dancing with the Stars." (Yet, they put some of these people on the show anyway.) My personal favorites are disco and Big Band.

For years I participated in a local entertainment production called the Red Glove Revue, a fundraiser for the Tulsa Cerebral Palsy Association. I found out about it through a friend who was on their board. They just don't do these types of galas anymore, and I was privileged to be a part of it for over four years. For one month of madness, dancers, singers, comedians, and wanna-be, but-still-very-entertaining jazzers and tappers practiced day and night in various venues around town who donated their facilities to us. The cast of every show was a mashup of accountants, bankers, doctors, insurance salespeople, secretaries, musicians, company CEO', stay-at-home moms and at least 2-3 pastors with talent we didn't even know about. TCPA always brought in a top director from New York to choreograph the event. The show was always presented close to Valentine's Day, so those January and early February trips to rehearsals were literally a chilling experience (especially in dance leotards and tights). The last one I did was six months after my daughter Sarah was born. We raised a lot of money while REDUCING our waistlines at the same time! I also made some great new friends every year while reconnecting with old ones.

Dating Websites

These are priceless. I actually had two former employers who met their wives on these sites. And yes, they're still together, and still happy! So if your love life is on pause, or even at a dead stop, these sites might fast-forward you to date that person who might ultimately become your MATE.

You really can experience plenty of "single jingle" if you use these sites correctly. I actually gave a membership to a single girlfriend one Christmas. She's still looking, but she's met some pretty interesting people, and having a great time doing it.

But beware, there are plenty of hilarious stories about de-lightful---and disastrous---dating experiences. So here's some advice for you to help ensure your jingle:

(1) **Post your real picture**. Not the one from 10 years and 20 pounds ago. Nothing says "I'll never call you again" than if your date stops you in a restaurant wanting you to be on the lookout for...YOU.

(2) **Be honest about likes and dislikes**. If you post a list of what you like based on what the cool guy or gal you're interested in loves to do, you're headed for e-dating dis-aster. You may find yourself backpacking in the Rockies instead of buying tickets to Broadway. Or diving when you'd rather be dancing. And if he or she asks you what books you like, don't say checkbooks. Even if it's true.

(3) **Take your own ride to your dating rendezvous**. This is as much a safety issue as a practical one. If it's ob-vious after some short conversation that this relationship has as much chance of taking off as an inebriated airline passenger talking their way through TSA, say your good-byes and hit the door...and the road. Having a friend send you a "rescue text" is another good escape.

Did you know there are lots of other dating sites BE-SIDES the ones who spend all the bucks on prime-time TV? If you've got a hobby, habit or hangup, there is a dating site for you. I've added my personal slogans and observations.

(1) **Purr-sonals**. For cat lovers. Purr- fect. You can sit and compare the virtues of Meow Mix versus Friskies, and discuss eco-friendly, yet chic, cat-litter box styles. I didn't see one for dog lovers' dating. Hey, this would be a site where saying your match was a "dog" would be a compliment. I'd name it the "Canine Connection...Love Gone To The Dogs."

(2) **Clown Dating**. Everyone loves a clown...let a clown love you. They say people who date awhile start to look alike. If both of you are clowns, you CAN!

(3) **Vampersonals** - You got it. If you are a vampire or go for gothic-looking guys or gals, this site is for you. It's sure to put a bite into your love life. (Or take one OUT of it.)

(4) **Salad Match**. For all you salad lovers. My idea for their slogan? "Lettuce Help You."

(5) **Darwin Dating**. They only accept THEIR definition of "beautiful people." Really. I see a lot of photoshopping that will happen here.

(6) **Sea Captain Date**. Specifically for ship captains---and people interested in dating them---the site helps them find other people who love the ocean as much as they do. If that's you, and you access this site, you could either be on the way to sea-ing the world, or having your spirits SINK after meeting who's on there!

(7) **Gluten-Free Singles**. So be sure that you find out if anything ELSE holds them together before that SECOND date!

(8) **Singles With Allergies**. That's great, but what if you're both allergic to the same things, and experience a simultaneous "allergen incident" because you both ate the same shellfish at that trendy seafood restaurant? Better get one of those emergency body monitors so the paramedics can find BOTH of you!

(9) **Hot Sauce Passions**. So you never have to worry about your first date saying "I don't like spicy food." Be sure you keep a stockpile of salsa in your purse or pantry to prove your taste for tangy cuisine.

(10) **Farmers Only.** So you can check out the best crop of people who love to harvest, hay and hoe as much as you do! Guys, want to impress? Show up for your first date in a stretch John Deere! Ladies, invite him to meet you at Cracker Barrel, and have him watch you prepare dinner for 20, after which you ring a dinner bell saying "come and get it." And then send everyone out to the front porch rockers afterward with coffee and pie.

(11) **BikerKiss.** Find that perfect Biker. He or she can turn out to be your Wheel of Fortune or really "chap" you the wrong way.

(12) **Ugly Schmucks**. For self-admitted people who feel they are ugly, but lovable.

For you single ladies reading this book, I think you are missing the boat: just marry a PIRATE CAPTAIN. Why? He owns his own transportation that doubles as a mobile home. He only needs ONE set of clothes. He doesn't need VISA Gold...He has the real thing. He can catch his own dinner. He can steal you all the jewelry you want. He'll plunder your enemies and/or the shopping mall of your choice. He only comes home every six months. And if you aren't looking for a long-term relationship, you might say he is short on life expectancy, but long on treasure chests.

Dog

Ok, cat lovers (yes, I love them too), dogs are still probably man's best friend. Over 50% of Americans prefer dogs as pets. Before you select YOUR new canine companion, however, you need to get seriously "Pup Close and Personal." Visit the shelter or breeding ranch where your potential paw-some new friend is, and find out as much as you can on the breeders AND the breed. (or BREEDS; you could have a Heinz 57, like a chihuahua, pug and poodle mix). I always go by my "MUTT" instinct; they make great pets. I was thinking you could name a dog Spam (when you don't know your dog's lineage or where he or she came from!) And be sure you know how big to expect your new friend to be; a Doberman and a beagle combination could still turn out to be over 100 pounds of pooch, and if your dog's new "forever home" is a 1,000-square foot apartment, this is not a good thing. You will have to rent them their OWN place. Talk about a DEPOSIT! And if you're looking for a guard dog, don't count on a pekinese and a pug combo to take a bite out of a burglar! (the laughter this bad guy may express at just seeing this pint-sized pooch patrol may be enough to get either your attention or that of the police who are looking for him.) If you want to buy a canine to train as a show dog, your new friend could take you from wags to riches!!! OK, so much for the pup talk.

My good friend Cheryl loves dogs as much as I do. She and her husband have three beautiful fur babies, a Great Pyrenee named Boomer, a Landseer Newfoundland named Mattie, and Izzie, their newest addition, a high-energy English Springer Spaniel, whom they teasingly call Izzie Busy Dizzy! And she understands what it's like to lose a pet. We suddenly lost our beloved cocker Monica last Thanksgiving weekend; she was the absolute sweetest, loving dog I think we had ever had. I loved posting her pictures and videos on Facebook, and I guess everyone else who saw them did too. Monica loved posing for the camera, especially when she had just been to see Ricki, her groomer. She would cock her head sideways at just the right angle to show off her coif! And Ricki always adorned her with the perfect seasonal scarves and ear bows; I still have all of them.

I finally was able to post about her loss on Facebook, and received amazing support from everyone, but particularly from Cheryl. We had a lengthy phone conversation the following week, and I'll never forget the encouraging things she said to me. We are finally starting to think about adopting another pet, and she's given us lots of ideas and advice. Thank you, my friend!

Dogs. These pooches are privileged! Think about the pros of BEING a dog:

If you have a wet nose, you're in GOOD health.

If you gain weight, it's someone else's fault.

Every garbage can is yet another cold buffet.

You can reach---and scratch---any part of yourself that itches...anytime, in public and without offending ANYONE!

You don't have to bathe yourself or even comb your own hair.

Dog Show

My favorite is the AKC National Dog Show on Thanksgiving Day. It immediately follows the Macy's Thanksgiving Day Parade. It's two hours of fur-filled festivities, during which viewers can watch over 200 canine contenders prance through their paces for some very highbrowed judges. I admire the dogs for tolerating being poked, primped, and paraded in the arena along with their paw-some competitors. And the NAMES they have. Sir Dash-A-Lot. Hairy Pawter. DOTUS (Dog of the United States). Droolius Caesar. Fluffernaut. And Rumor. When this German Shepherd won Best in Show at the Westminster dog show in February, the judges announced, "Rumor has it." Because he literally DID.

I also find it interesting that many of these dogs LOOK like their owners. Like the lady with hair so tightly permed that it looked like a cotton candy hat instead of hair, who was strolling with her equally poofed-out poodle. Or the 6' tall, long-haired slim woman with large brown eyes parading through the dog park with her Afghan.

If you're looking for a new pet, you can find out everything you want about any breed there is. If you already have a pet, jingle knowing that yours costs a lot less to care for than these guys--and gals--do. Want some more jingle? Put your FURRY friends in front of the TV that day and watch THEIR response! I've seen hilarious videos on this on YouTube...make your own to share with family and friends! Yes, cats love it too! (It gives them attack strategy ideas to inflict on the dog in their life.)

E

Ebay

The ultimate experience in "Day Trading"...A day shopping on Ebay. Now that's "jingle." You can buy anything your little jingle heart desires. From antiques to autos, from hats to hot tubs, It's all in the bidding. What I can't hold AT bay while on E-Bay is my desire to charge, charge, charge!!

Empty Nesting

Now here's some serious jingle to look forward to. While every year thousands of parents send their last child off to college with tearful goodbyes, they're secretly CELEBRATING. Think about all the jingle you can now enjoy:

1. You can host a Zumba class in your new "exercise room."

2. You buy groceries Tuesday and still have most of them Wednesday.

3. You can stay out late yourself, instead of waiting on your kids who are.

4. Socks match for the first time in ten years.

5. Your water bill reduces because your laundry load does.

6. The question "what's for dinner" is no longer spoken.

7. You can walk all around the house without tripping on a skateboard or empty pizza boxes.

8. When the kids come back to visit, you fix them one meal, and then hand them your broken Ipads and PCs to fix.

9. You no longer have a monthly visit from your city's Haz-Mat team.

10. You no longer have to hide the wine, car keys or your favorite sweater.

Enter a Contest

From your best guacamole recipe to writing a new jingle for toilet paper (We Follow Our Butt Instincts in Everything We Do, or how about TipTop TP: Our Success Is On A Roll or, Just Roll With It...yes, I really wrote these for a contest), from why you deserve a trip to Jamaica or ice cream for life, entering a contest can present all KINDS of jingle opportunities. Like money. If you enter competitions that test your knowledge or skills, you increase your chances of winning; plus, you could make some serious cash! Publisher's Clearing House doesn't take much effort (peeling and sticking labels doesn't take a lot of time or brainpower, but you also have less than one in a 300 million chance of winning.)

If not money, you could win recognition in your chosen hobby or work field. Or just do it just for the sheer jingle of doing it. A major national drugstore chain offers incentives to do focus group surveys via email; you get big discounts off merchandise they want you to evaluate and additional store rewards points too. I save up all mine over the year, and cash them in at Christmas. I cashed in points totaling over $200 worth last year.

Make a home video featuring kids or pets and submit it to any one of a number of TV video contest shows. From *America's Funniest Home Videos* to *Funniest Pets and People*, and everything in between, there are plenty of jingle opportunities out there. Why kids and pets? Because they're ALWAYS doing something wild; you just need to be ready to film it! Catch it, and you just might be able to cash in on their craziness. One pet food company does a Halloween costume contest every October. What I like as much as the costumes is the LOOKS the pets give their owners, i.e., the revenge they are planning on you later on, and when you least expect it.

I once won the City Spelling Bee contest in my hometown. I went to state, and took third place. The guy who beat me and another girl won the national title. I won $50, a set of encyclopedias, and a free day out of school. Doesn't sound like a lot? Tell you what; from that point on, I only had to use spell-check as a BACKUP. And that really cute guy in my eighth grade history class finally realized I existed.

If you choose to audition for *The Voice* or *America's Got Talent*, be sure you have an IDENTIFIABLE gift for whichever contest you enter. It really gets boring seeing people who make a profession out of throwing up on national TV or hearing a voice that sounds like a rapper with whooping cough.

By the way, gambling is not a contest. It's a tug of war. Between you and the casino house...for YOUR MONEY.

Your mission at a gambling casino---should you choose to accept it---is to LOSE as LITTLE as possible. Most of us will hear a lot less jingle in our pockets if we spend much time there. And don't wager any more money than you can afford to lose. Because most of the time you WILL lose it! And if you are lucky enough TO win any amount of money, just RUN!! (well, cash out first). And frankly, the easiest way to double your money is just fold it in half and put it back in your pocket.

Exercise

The only real jingle I get out of exercise is figuring out creative ways to NOT do it! But forget sweating to the oldies---or any other music decade---and try my personal workout wonders! You can really burn some calories, with a minimum of "sweat equity."

1. **The Sip-Up**. Lift up your coffee cup. At 10 sips per cup x 3 cups/day, that's 10,950 sips a year. If the cup weighs 1/2 pound, that's 5,475 pounds of sip-strengthening activity per year.

2. **The Shoe Stretch**. Reaching under the bed to get your shoes at least 4 times a day. That's 1,460 sole stretches per year.

3. **The Laundry Lift**. At an average of 25 pounds a week, that's 1,300 pounds of basket pressing a year.

4. **The Elevator Push**. How many times you can push an elevator button without getting winded.

5. **The Dialer Dash** . Run, don't walk, to answer the phone at least four times a day. That's 1,460 times a year. If you spend ten minutes a day doing it, that's 3,650 minutes a year, or over 60 hours!

6. **Gem-Shorts**. Short, quick up and down movements of your fingers while wearing good jewelry.

7. **Call Catching.** Switching your phone back and forth from ear to ear during the day on every phone call. Assuming an average of 20 calls a day, that's 7,300 swings a year using a 1/4-pound weight. You'll be tossing to the tune of 1,825 pounds a year. So lose some weight while you're waiting for that client to answer your questions on that new contract or your kids to tell you about their latest college disaster. Land line phones are extra credit; they're heavier.

So don't have a physical fit. Exercise can be FUN!

F

Facebook

Ok, who CAN'T get some jingle from Facebook posts?

Facebook is your internet scrapbook, social calendar, and a sharing place for your pics, platform, philosophy, pet peeves, even politics with your friends...or the world! It's like a "one-stop shop" for sharing your LIFE. This amazing technology allows you to do everything from "Fund Me" to "Friend Me." You can use Facebook for your inspiration, information, and even insinuation (be careful what you say!) Express admiration, admonition and even ask for advice from your friends (or from anyone else who's willing to reply!) You can raise money, raise eyebrows, ... OR even raise a little CAIN!

What gives so much jingle to me on Facebook is what people are willing to post, and why they think it's important...to ANYONE. Some of the funniest I've seen...

1) A woman posts a long list of culinary dishes, including pictures, that she's considering making for dinner, accompanied by reasons her husband probably won't like them.

2) A professional thief posts a resume.

3) A poster asks for prayer requests...that she'll get enough money to pay her Macy's bill before her husband finds out. She chose to SHARE this little tidbit with her friends. Her husband, who had coincidentally just created his own page the same day, later posted an "unlike" followed by a long line of well, let's say, rather "expressive" emojis. Earth to Facebookers: Remember that on Facebook you and your significant other are VERY likely to have a lot of MUTUAL friends. Interesting...this lady mysteriously quit posting pics of her new shoes and doorbuster coupons. Hmmm...

4) A mom posts pics of her toddler's "poop premiere."

5) A mom posts a complete timeline of her day, including naps and pics of her picking up drive-through Wendy's.

6) The female half of a retired couple posts a "Taster's Choice" style daily chronicle of their lives, including colorful commentary on their neighbors, their dogs and all the places her husband instantly falls asleep around the house. (on the computer, while talking, on the commode).

What I REALLY enjoy on Facebook are:

(1) Videos of soldiers returning home from duty reuniting with family and friends...and their PETS. Keep Kleenex handy; you'll need it.

(2) People celebrating landmark birthdays. (favorite: 95 year old woman dancing with a professional instructor to "Stayin Alive")

(3) People triumphing over illness or tragedy to inspire others.

(4) Vintage dance videos with modern music behind them.

(5) Children trying to talk like grownups.

(6) Good recipes.

(7) Funny pet videos. My favorite was the cat who had figured out how to climb up to the pet food cabinet, open the door, and pull out dinner for herself and all her feline friends waiting below! Or the two cats who were passing the milk bowl back and forth trying to decide who owned it.

(8) The woman who did the Star Wars' Chewy character imitation in her car while waiting to pick up her kids from school. (one of my favorites!)

But think about it. If you applied Facebook principles to making friends in person, you might have problems. Say you stop someone on the street and start telling them what you ate today, how you feel (complete with the matching facial expression), what you did last night and what you plan to do later---and with whom---you might have a problem. You start giving them pictures of you and your family at Christmas, on vacation, watering the grass, playing with your dog, and other life activities. You listen to their conversations, and give them a thumbs-up to let them know that you like them. And it works! You will soon find YOURSELF being followed...by your local police department, someone's private detective, possibly a psychiatrist, or the ultimate...a process server holding a restraining order.

Family

We all need family for more jingle in our lives. No matter what foolish things we've done, our family still loves us unconditionally. So if you think you just need your family for: (1) bail money, (2) organ donor, (3) bank, (4) pharmacy or (5) a place to crash until you find your "dream" digs, you need to reevaluate your priorities. Family are who instilled in us our values, and gave us our foundation to live by. Families are like branches on a tree; we may all grow in different directions, but our ROOTS are still the same! And don't use the fact your family does not have email, Twitter or Instagram as a reason not to stay connected. And if they do have e-mail, don't count a typed message to their "address" as a visit home. If you want to "update your status," GO to their ACTUAL address and do it in person!

Flash Mobs

Attend one, organize one or PARTICIPATE in one for a good cause...or just for fun! Any way you do it, you'll get jingle...or give some!

The best ones I 've seen:

(1) Choir in shopping mall doing the Hallelujah Chorus from Handel's Messiah.

(2) Symphony orchestra doing Pachelbel's Canon on a city street.

(3) Hip-hop Dancers helping a very nervous man propose at Disney World.

(4) Doctors and nurses singing Michael Jackson song "Beat It" at a cancer care hospital.

(5) Santas singing "Santa Claus is coming to Town"at a children's hospital.

(6) Train riders doing a Riverdance rendition at a river cruise terminal.

(7) "Flight attendants" doing Disco Inferno, Rollin on the River at the airport. And Up, Up and Away for a finale.

Best One I've Done:

(1) Jazz Dance routine performed to songs with the word "Heart" in their song titles. With ten other women

from several radio and TV stations at a local mall here in town, we dressed up as hearts and danced our "hearts" OUT to draw awareness and financial support for the local branch of the American Heart Association. Some of the songs? Heart and Soul, Don't Go Breaking My Heart, Put a Little Love In Your Heart, How to Mend A Broken Heart, Achy Breaky Heart and Queen of Hearts. (I still have those red heels- see "Keepsake.")

The postscript to this heart event nearly stopped mine, when I suddenly heard the wail of a police siren behind me as I was heading for home. Keep in mind I was STILL wearing my costume. First, I had no seatbelt, as the "heart" that covered my torso kept me from being able to fasten it. And, it stuck out in front of me just enough that I had to push my seat back to be able to drive. My feet could just reach the accelerator and brake. The officer said he stopped me because a passing driver had seen me, calling in with a report of a red alien heading south on Sheridan Road. And frankly, to him I looked like an escapee from Sing-A-Gram or a cardiologists' convention booth.

Fishing

Go ahead, get hooked!... on this American classic sport. Remember, there's water SOMEWHERE! Whether it's a pond, river, lake or a REALLY big puddle, do it! You may not "reel" in anything but scraggly weeds or a soggy sneaker for your efforts, but you're sure to catch a "reel"-ly great time just being with family and friends. You don't have to have any skills whatsoever; I'm living proof of that. My "Catch of the Day" could only be served at a restaurant as an appetizer. Or they could promote Hush Puppies as the main course with a trout GARNISH. Yes, I can say the only good thing I've gotten "on line" is a new cocktail dress. My favorite fishing sign was on a highway just a mile from a popular anglers' hangout, which said, "Warning: Fish Stories Ahead." And there were. I just didn't have any. Fish only come in three sizes: S, M and G. Small, Medium and Got Away. I always had #3. But even though I got baited more than once to go, I always had a great time.

Fly

Go up, up and away at least once in your lifetime. As common as flying is, less than half of Americans have taken a commercial or private airplane ride. It's a lot like that in life. I like to call it Flight Life. Be sure your Attitude is locked and in the upright position. All self-destructive devices should be turned off and put away: negativity, hurt and discouragement. If you experience loss of altitude during this flight, reach up and pull down Prayers. Prayers are activated by Faith, and once activated, you can help other passengers on the flight with you. And NO BAGGAGE allowed on board.

My mom was terrified of flying. So much that, upon being offered a trip to Hawaii as an anniversary gift by my dad, she immediately started checking on BOAT sailings from LA. Dad simply told her that if she wasn't flying, she wasn't going. They figured it out. Dad took her to her doctor on Thursday, filled a Valium prescription on Friday, and boarded the plane on Saturday. So she became calm enough to get TO the plane, and even calmer after they visited the second floor cocktail lounge once she was ON the plane. My dad would only comment later that she and three ladies from New Jersey entertained the passengers with "I Did It My Way", "Leaving On A Jet Plane", and "Fly Away With Me"...multiple times on the trip over. Upon arriving, the flight crew took off ...to their OWN bar.

As you know, planes have to be maintained to be ABLE to fly, and you can really get some jingle just knowing some of the things pilots report, and the real response they get back from maintenance engineers.

(1) Right inside main tire almost needs replacement.

Almost replaced inside front tire.

(2) Dead bugs on windshield.

Live bugs on order.

(3) Suspected crack in windshield.

Suspect you're right.

(4) Number 3 engine missing.

Number 3 engine found after brief search.

(5) Aircraft handles funny.

Aircraft instructed to straighten up, fly right and be serious.

(6) Target radar hums.

Reprogrammed target radar with lyrics.

(7) Mouse in cockpit.

Cat installed.

(8) Something loose in the galley.

Something tightened in the galley.

Food

Let's face it, eating great food is a real jingle-maker. Especially when enjoyed with friends and family. I recently found out some pretty great things about food. If you believe it all, you can break up with your pharmacy, because the cure for whatever you've got is in the produce department at your local grocery store! From headaches to hemorrhoids, nerves to nephritis, there's a fruit for it!

For instance, how about THESE medical miracles...

1. Pineapples — Burns fat.
2. Bananas — Fights viruses
3. Cauliflower — Helps the kidneys.
4. Fennel — Pain reliever
5. Sweet potatoes — Reduces IBS.
6. Blueberries — Balances blood sugar
7. Apples — Relieves anxiety
8. Lemons — Cleanses the liver

Well, as far as the vegetables go, I'd name this cure the "Veg-O-<u>MAGIC</u>."

On the fruits? I'd call it the Citrus Connection...The Cure For The Common Anything.

Now, this is all well and good, but my question is: If you're dealing with anxiety, depression, constipation AND a headache at the same time, how DO you pack all that produce into your purse or PC case? You don't. I can see it now, you just wear a produce PATCH. And I now know why there's an apple on the teacher's desk, and students are always gifting apples to them; their nerves are SHOT! Solution: Plant an orchard! That way, these exhausted educators can just reach out the door and grab a bite of bliss any time they want.

A few more things that will keep you jingling about food if you follow the rules. Common food myths you need to remember are:

1. Trying to eat anything at one sitting that you cannot lift will not produce the desired results.

2. A one-pound tomato does NOT have fewer calories than a 3-ounce apple turnover.

3. Food doesn't have fewer calories because you don't like it, but choose to eat it anyway.

4. Low-calorie does not mean NO calorie.

5. Eating "clean" does NOT mean you simply wash your food first.

Forgiveness

When someone hurts you, write out the hurt in sand, so it can be washed away and forgotten. When someone does something good for you, write the kindness in stone so that you will always remember it. Forgiving people for the past is the only way to keep the jingle in your future. Never sacrifice your class to get even with someone who has none. Take the high road; let them take the gutter.

Friends

...are the family you pick for yourself. Friends are the people in your life who, when you have made a total fool of yourself, don't feel like you've done a permanent job. A real friend is the one who walks in when the rest of the world walks out, who believes in you when you have stopped believing in yourself. It takes a very long time to grow an old friend. Friends don't like you BECAUSE, they love you ALTHOUGH. Even Abraham Lincoln said, "The better part of one's life consists of his friend-ships." A hug is worth a thousand words; A friend is worth much more. I was a Girl Scout for several years, and they had a lot to say about friends; it's even a part of their motto. "Make new friends and keep the old, one is silver and the other gold."

I meet a lot of people during my daily life. I like to think of strangers as friends just waiting to happen. For me, friends are the bacon bits in life's salad bowl. They season it and give it color and flavor. I love to go shopping for antiques; but the most treasured thing "old" I possess are old FRIENDS. Friends are like four-leaf clovers; hard to find and very lucky to have.

I met a very special friend I've only had come into my life over the past three years. She was one of those strangers. Semi-retired from a local newspaper, she was thinking about writing a cookbook, and took a job at Reasor's to learn more about foods. From desserts to dips to soups and sauces, Luci worked at various stand setups throughout the store. A creative genius, I came to find out as I got to know her, she had amazing ways to describe these new culinary delicacies (even if it was only a new brand of baked beans), and knew just how to entice store customers to try a taste...just ONCE. Once they did, they scurried down to the aisle where the product was...and bought almost every time. You could see her Irish red hair shining like a beacon of invitation almost as soon as you walked in. Her enthusiasm was contagious, and I started stopping to visit with her. As I found out, she was a journalist, had similar education, and even knew some of the same people I did. I told her to contact me about publicizing her new book, and then we both wound up critiquing each other's books when I wrote my first one. Now we both use the same editor, and have breakfast every month to talk books. I would never have had this wonderful friend if I had not taken the time to reach out.

G

Garage Sale

Regardless of your gender, everyone can jingle their way through a good garage sale. I call it Jingle By The Yard. No matter where you live, SOMEONE is having one. And if you want a list, just check Craigslist, the classifieds in your local paper, or even signs in your neighborhood. Whether the hosts are moving in, moving out, downsizing, need some extra cash, or getting rid of Junior's baseball uniforms or Hubby's Star Trek toys, their trash can be YOUR treasure.

And you won't BELIEVE the treasures you will find...and how CHEAP you can find them.

One of my best personal stories is about a garage sale I attended in my neighborhood a few years ago. As I was browsing through the usual books, clothes and garden tools that lined most of the driveways, I saw a beautiful set of white china marked with a raised gray lace-like overlay. It was a service for eight, and the seller had it priced at $25. I needed china like a hole in the head, but these were so striking that I had to pick up one of the dishes to see where it was made, fully expecting to see a Made in Japan decal because of the asking price.

What met my eyes was no less than amazing. I saw the stamp of a famous Bavarian factory on the bottom. I walked over to the wife and told her, "I would love to have this, but you don't want to sell this to me or anyone for just $25." When she asked why, I told her what I had just pulled up on my smartphone about this factory. I wrote down the name of a reputable antique dealer in the area I knew and suggested she give him a call. She was very grateful, and found out that these dishes were worth a WHOLE lot more. And because they also had some beautiful Civil War period pieces, he appraised those for her too. I had never met her before that day, but we have stayed in touch all this time since they moved away. I would have loved to have those dishes, but I loved helping this woman so much more. I guess that was a day I really got my jingle by giving it away. (because I'll never find that price again!)

And even if you don't buy anything at these driveway dealers, you can get some jingle just by seeing what people are willing to sell.

(1) Aquarium WITH fish.

(2) A dog. (because they were moving and couldn't take him)

(3) A cat. (See #2)

(4) A Beatles signed first album. (Meet the Beatles)

(5) A vintage NCR cash register.

(6) Football tickets.

(7) A collection of Mountain Dew bottle caps.

(8) A Model-T.

(9) A set of war medals.

(10) Vera Wang wedding gown.

(11) A neon "Open" sign.

(12) A high-school term paper on the effects of Global Warming.

(13) Used sport socks.

(14) Miss Piggy and Kermit wedding collectibles.

(15) Empty wine bottles.

(16) Gasoline pump.

(17) Set of police handcuffs.

(18) Used toilet seat.

Give

Give...of your time, talent and treasure, whenever and however you can. And as often as you can. Giving to others can GET a lot of jingle into your heart.

However, for CERTAIN gifts, please use some judgment. Take Mother's Day. Nothing says "I Love You" like a Walgreen's plastic bag containing a box of Q-tips, batteries, a Twix candy bar and a $1 recycled card. (And putting a bow on the bag does NOT make it any more appealing.) Yet that same box of batteries will power

Dad's TV remote for a year; so wait a month. Add a subscription to NFL Sunday Ticket, and you're home free for Father's Day.

Some gifts you can make are so special, I just had to share them here. Try doing this for each of your children. Start a scrapbook their first year of school, and at the end of each grade, have your child's favorite teachers pen a few lines about them. Stash it someplace until they're ready to graduate. Give it to them as part of their high school graduation present. It is the most precious gift they will ever receive. (with better future predictions than career guidance counselors!)

A gift I started giving myself many years ago is a garden. No, not flats full of those live flowers I have to plant and water constantly, but a PICTURE garden. (I do have the real thing, though). I took---and still take---photos of every bouquet of flowers my husband, friends or family have sent to me over the years and put them into a scrapbook; and then, I made copies of as many as I could and created a posie print collage I framed and put in our master bedroom. The memory of the occasions and the beauty of the blossoms stays with me forever.

My friend Barb gave me a very special gift I particularly treasure. Both of our dads worked for Phillips Petroleum, and a couple of years ago she gave me a collection of Philips memorabilia and crystal, playing cards, a cigarette lighter, tape measure and other items.

My friends Amy and Tami have both each shared special pieces of their moms' jewelry collections with me.

One gift I GAVE I particularly remember; it was a RESERVATION. My boss at Stephens Media was finally meeting---live and in person---the lady he had met online on eHarmony. After four months of texting, talking and Skyping, she was finally going to be able to come to town...ON VALENTINE'S DAY. This nervous suitor had tried in vain for three days to get a reservation---anywhere---and was pretty down about it, with only two days to go. I made a call to my husband, and we both agreed; we would give him our reservation at the restaurant we went to every year, the one where Bob had proposed. Somehow we felt this would give them good luck. I walked into his office with the owner's name and cell number written on the back of my business card; Mark was overwhelmed. Suffice it to say, from what the restaurant owner told us to the telling look on Mark's face the next day, we knew it was a good move. He proposed to her a month later, they married three months later, and have been married for seven years.

Grocery Store

OK, you ask, how in the world do you get jingle going to the grocery store? Just ask my husband. He shops for groceries like I shop for clothes. For him, it's much more about entertainment than it is about eating. He goes to just pick up some ham and cheese (SURE you are, dear) and brings back the whole deli...plus four kinds of bread. Because I do the majority of the SERIOUS food shopping at our house, I have to clean my pantry out every month because of all of the "mystery merchandise" that keeps showing up in there. He's one of those people who COLLECT food as opposed to actually CONSUMING it. Like his horde of salad dressings. He is so proud of his Buffalo Ranch, Santa Fe, Raspberry Vinaigrette and Parmesan Caesar. All different brands. And in very colorful packaging. He thinks the names are cool, and lines them up in there like his own personal set of salad condiments, but never uses them. I'm convinced he just likes the fact he HAS them.

I'm no less guilty in another area of my life. Kind of like the clothes I buy from time to time on impulse, suffer buyer's remorse the next day---or the next HOUR---but then don't want to take them back, because SURELY I will find SOMEPLACE to wear them SOMETIME. I could open my own store in my garage with what I DON'T wear. It gets worse; I have a summer AND a winter closet. And a separate closet for SHOES. But at least you can RETURN clothes. Food is an entirely different thing. They ask a LOT more questions.

Back to my husband, I especially like it when he returns from the GROCERY store without one grocery ITEM. I return home to find a countertop covered with bags of batteries. Switchplate covers. Two-pack of toilet brushes. Windex. Rubber bands. Motor oil. The newest As Seen on TV gadget or gizmo. Fireplace matches. Dental floss. Bird seed. After I said something about it, he wanted to be sure I couldn't say that again, so he always picks up one token bag of Nacho Cheese Doritos.

Grocery shopping has other hazards, but I call them jingle opportunities. My favorite store occasionally has birds fly in through the automatic doors. It's jingle just watching the staff trying to chase them out. I actually watched a customer bombarded with a "deposit" from a swooping sparrow just as he opened a door in frozen foods. He thought he was picking up Birds' Eye frozen corn. Well, He got another part.

A little piece of advice for you: Don't ever go grocery shopping hungry. Or you may find yourself the proud OWNER of Aisle 4.

Don't forget checkout. The "pay pad" conducts an extensive interview with you and your credit or debit card before you are allowed to leave.

1. Do you have a pin?

2. Enter it.

3. Is this the correct amount? (oh, so the price is NEGOTIABLE?)

4. Do you want cash back? (Sure I would, is this a gift?)

5. If yes, enter amount.

6. Now, Is THIS cashback amount correct?

7. Is the cashback amount plus your store total correct?

......and what I'm waiting for is: (wait for it)

8. Is this your FINAL answer?

And heaven help you if you want to write a check. A store riot is sure to ensue because of the extra two minutes it takes.

And what's REALLY fun? You use your debit card, and the next time you enter the store and swipe the card, the machine already KNOWS YOUR PIN. This is not a good thing. And this same major retail store chain has the highest incidences of credit card fraud. I've gone through four new debit cards in three years. Wonder why.

H

Hair

Regardless of your gender, new hair can really raise your self-image jingle. For all the ladies reading this book, hair appointments are definitely a MANE event, every bit as crucial to your personal jingle-being as those doctor, dental, and investment banker visits. I schedule my hair appointments months in advance, and BE-FORE I schedule anything else. Hey, we all know we need to be particular about who we choose to maintain our health and wealth. For you ladies, who's in charge of your COIFFURE is #3 on the list! That person is your Coiffure Concierge! A great hair stylist can put your self-image jingle over the top. Nicole certainly does that for me: if she ever moves out of town, I will have to buy a second home wherever she lives. Her name is Nicole; that's Christmas jingle in itself (the female version of Nick, St. Nicholas, you get it), so I know I've made the right decision.

I've even coined a new term: hairography: the science of deciding WHERE to put the highlights. A new cut, color and style can literally change your appearance...AND your jingle! Plus, to the ladies, an ADDED bonus; great hair REALLY sets off our tiaras! And for those of us who are frankly over 50...stick to wearing the color pink in your threads, NOT your tresses.

Hallmark Channel

It's my go-to "jingle-on-demand" TV channel all year, especially during the holidays. This network celebrates all the pluses and positives in life. It's what most of us want our lives to be. Someone told me once that watching this channel is like living in La La Land. Well, if it is, I want to buy up as much of THIS real estate as I can! Reality is tough enough. Who wants to see 24/7 violence, whether real or rigged? Escape---if only for a little while---to some joy and jingle. They say that you become what you see, and I believe it. I become happy and full of hope and jingle when I watch this channel. I DVR the new Christmas movies every December, and watch them anytime I need a jingle boost!

Halloween Party

Nothing beats a great Halloween dress-up party. Or just dress up at home for your own "spook-tacular" evening. It's a way you can be totally someone---or some-THING---else for one magical night. My favorite outfit a couple ever wore to a Halloween party: they called it 20/20. They sewed together two green work jumpsuits, then painted a gi-normous eye in the middle of two motorcycle helmets. Ahhh, Halloween: I have not yet begun to fright!!

Home

It's not only where the heart is, it's your haven away from an increasingly crazy, mixed up world that we're living in. Spend as much time with your family there as you can. And when you have to be away, home is not a place, but a FEELING that you carry with you. The real test of home is not how you feel when you're there, but what you feel as soon as you LEAVE. And a feeling that gives you jingle. So much that you can't wait to get back!!

Texas real estate investor and "Blue Collar Millionaire" Ron Sturgeon knew the importance of home, especially after he saw the massive devastation in Garland, Texas caused by massive tornadoes that hit the area in 2016. With two properties valued at over $1 million each that his company had up for sale in the area, he decided to lease the houses to affected families---for $1 per month---instead of pursuing buyers. Because he started his own adult life homeless, with only $1,500 in his pocket and a one-half interest in a rusted-out Volkswagen, he knew about poverty and loss, saw the chance to give back...and DID. When you gather around your Christmas tree each December, remember that it's not what's UNDER the tree that's important, but what people are AROUND it that matter.

Hobby

Hobbies are those wonderful activities we CHOOSE do when we're not working or doing those life things we HAVE to do. In my case, my work is one my biggest hobbies: a hobby with pay. Writing creative marketing campaigns for businesses is a major jingle opportunity. Seeing them succeed as a result of that makes me literally jingle all over. Whatever your own jingle-maker is, do it! But don't let your hobby turn into hoarding! You don't want people to mistake your front yard for a Goodwill collection center.

A lot of people choose art as a hobby. A client of mine owns a stained glass and art studio that's been a landmark business here in metro Tulsa for over 40 years. He's one of the lucky ones; his business is also his hobby, so he goes to his studio jingle-filled every day. Whether you view it, create it or buy it for your home or office, art produces a jingle in our hearts and minds that is indisputable. So whether you choose to paint, plaster, solder or glaze, it's a jingle experience you won't want to miss.

But there are a lot of people out there who think they really have professional art "talent," when what I see on a painting at their show looks like "Beginning Vandalism;" you know, when the painting looks like it's been mugged!

I particularly love it when people "wear" their hobby interest on their apparel. **My favorites:**

One of my handcrafting friends has a shirt with "Knit Happens" on it. A boating enthusiast client proudly wears a "Got Yacht?" slicker when he's out to sea. Or, how about "Gem"-Nastics, sported by a friend who designs jewelry. And lest us not forget "The Train Whisperer." There's a host of others I could name here.

Hope

Hope is that perennial optimism that gives us reason to get up every day. If things are great, we hope that they continue. If they're not, we hope they will get better. Whatever your belief in a higher power is, having hope can help you weather life's storms and reach the calm on the other side. So, practice being positive.

Hugs

A simple hug is one of the simplest, most meaningful ways you can give people jingle...without saying a word. It's a proven fact that hugging someone at least twice a day will add an average of eight years to your life. And hugs convey your feelings regardless of why they're given. A hug of congratulations to a new bride. A hug of consolation to your child who just fell off her bike. A hug of support to a co-worker as he steps on the stage for that big presentation. A hug of pride to your daughter at her college graduation. A hug of comfort to a grieving friend at a funeral. That wonderful, warm fuzzy feeling lasts far beyond the less-than-a-minute time it takes to do it. If my arms won't reach the people I care about, I still hug them with my prayers.

I

Ice Cream

Who DOESN'T love ice cream? In the cone, in a dish, or even in a cake, ice cream can give you frozen jingle like nothing else on the planet. You can solve all the world's problems while consuming this cold confection. Whether it's chocolate, vanilla, Rocky Road, or Bubblegum, it's a real jingle-starter! (Just be sure you don't WEAR more of it than you EAT.) It's a great attitude adjustor for kids as well; sure beats putting them in time out; and since you're paying for it, YOU get to have some too.

Ice Skating

Lace up a pair of ice skates and go out for a "spin" at least once in your lifetime. Your first time may be your last---as it was for me---but at least you can say you did

it. Want an easy way to go ice skating? WATCH it......
on TV. All of the speed, none of the spills! Plus, you
don't have to diet constantly to fit into those itty bitty
costumes.

Imagine

If you are strong enough to imagine it, you CAN jingle
your way to becoming it! One of my favorite en-
trepreneurs was Walt Disney. He was told his ideas were
unrealistic and unattainable, and that he would never
amount to anything in his life. Now that the very fa-
miliar Cinderella's castle logo graces theme parks, movie
screens, cruise ships, toy labels, and a number of charities. Disney proved that the answer to the question: "Are
you a man or a mouse?" was that he was BOTH. And he
built an incredible empire because he saw a vision of not
what WAS, but what COULD be. You can think of your
imagination as life's coming attractions that YOU create.

Instant

These days, we live in an "instant" society. Instant coffee.
Instant food. Instant money. Instant access to the world
through the internet. (Hey, it's the only place you can
"speed" without getting a ticket!) And we love it. It gives

us jingle. But sometimes we just need to turn our lives down to simmer and slow-cook our time we have on this earth to appreciate what's really important. Because of the name of my business (The Ad Genie), sometimes customers get the impression I can truly make marketing results happen instantly! My response always is: "I like to think I'm pretty good. But I'm not THAT good. So give me at least until Friday."

Invent

... a new ANYTHING. A new way of driving down a one-way street the wrong way without a collision. A new recipe for Spam. It can even be a creative new trick to get rid of telemarketers. Like telling them in your best police detective voice that they have just called into an active crime scene, and say, "Soooo...how do YOU know _____(your name here). And be sure to stay on the line until my sergeant can verify your identity for the investigation." My favorite that I just created: The "Applause App." Sixty minutes of non-stop applause punctuated by "encouragisms:" Way to Go! Congratulations! Don't worry! The diet worked! You look so thin in those jeans! You're on Publisher's Clearing House's short list! You'll get that promotion! You look at least ten years longer than you are! For $20 more, you can have the app personalized.

Invite

... neighbors or friends over for a spontaneous get-to-gether. I call it a Street Social. By opening your home (or your yard, garage, porch or sidewalk), you give jingle to others, and jingle yourself in the process. And it can be for any reason, and at any time. Morning donuts and coffee for the frazzled, bleary-eyed moms in your block after the bus leaves. Afternoon tea on the back patio or front porch on a hot summer Saturday. Ice cream cones in your driveway. Or because It's Wednesday. Your computer virus is cured. You got the coffee stain out of your husband's Bee Gees Tribute shirt. You want to throw a launch party for your sprinkler system. The online order dress you got in the mail FITS. Or just because you want to celebrate having these great people in your life. Jingle a little more and invite the new family in the neighbor-hood you haven't met, a senior who doesn't get out much, and especially a veteran.

We had a very hasty "Tornado Watch" street social last year; however, we were social just long enough to deter-mine that we all needed to become very social, very quickly with our inside bathrooms. The funnel was only a few miles north and appeared to be heading directly for us. My carpet cleaner guys had just finished up, and I of-fered to share our jacuzzi. Now THAT would have made quite a Facebook post. "Stanley Steemer Shelters with

Jittery Customer in Jacuzzi To Avoid Clean Sweep by Tornado." Especially since my husband was out getting a haircut four miles away, and had been herded into their back room for shelter...a place with no cell phone reception. I just didn't have the time---at the time---to focus on creating a Kodak moment. I was more worried that our house would BECOME a Kodak moment for the six o'clock news. As it turned out, the tornado turned east and missed us.

J

Job

If your current job's not a jingle, make the one you have as jingle-filled as possible. Strive to be the very best at whatever work you do until you find something that DOES ring your bell. Even if you work as food-taster, dog walker, or in a call center as some type of customer service representative. My favorite is an incontinence care specialist...I mean, what DO you say to people who call in? Because the only three things you can talk about are: size, absorbency and gender of the caller. I mean, they can't fix leaks; they can only provide a means to "deal with the dribble."

I sold health and life insurance for about a year. And as people who know me know how much I love Top Ten lists, I already had dozens of absolutely outrageous answers---within the first month of working there---that customers gave me to questions asked during a routine insurance application. But I'll share the best ones. These REALLY happened. You just can't make this stuff up.

(1) Do you have a nervous disorder? Yes. It happens every day about 3 p.m. ...when the kids come home.

(2) No, sir, international coverage does not include any trips outside the earth's atmosphere.

(3) No, sir, "operations during the past five years" does not refer to the number of missions you did with the CIA.

(4) No, ma'am, we can't list your boa constrictor as a dependent.

(5) Well, I'm only BARELY pregnant.

(6) Blue Coverage Premier does not mean you get tickets to red carpet movie openings.

(7) No, ma'am, we can't debit your gambling account at the Golden Nugget Casino for your insurance premium.

(8) Yes, sir, we DO consider bunji jumping over the Grand Canyon a hazardous sport. Please tell me you don't do that.

(9) Well, my wife says I ACT old enough to be on Medicare.

(10) I don't take any medications. I'm thinking about calling my doctor, though. I keep hearing these voices...

Working hard at something you don't care about is stress. Working at something you LOVE is called passion. Find YOUR passion...and you'll find your jingle as well.

And here's another reason you want to do well at any job you have. Your don't want your boss recording THESE comments on ANY of your performance appraisals:

(1) If you give him a penny, you'd get change back.

(2) Some drink from the fountain of knowledge; this woman only gargled.

(3) He has a photographic memory, but with the lens cover glued on.

(4) This person would argue with a signpost.

(5) He has a knack for making strangers immediately.

(6) The gates are down, the lights are flashing, but the train just isn't coming.

(7) She doesn't have ulcers, but she's a carrier.

(8) This young woman has delusions of adequacy.

(9) Since my last report, this employee has reached rock bottom and has started to dig.

(10) She sets low working standards and consistently fails to achieve them.

(11) This employee should go far, and the sooner he starts, the better.

(12) This employee is depriving a village somewhere of an idiot.

Looking for something TOTALLY different to do for employment? Try these:

(1) Luggage lock tester.

(2) Greeting card writer.*

(3) Private investigator.*

(4) Nail Polish Namer.

(5) Pick-Up Instructor. (help for shy men wanting to meet women)

(6) Golf Ball Diver.*

(7) Fake Facebooker for Hire. (create fake pages to sell something, impress a member of the opposite sex, and who knows what else)

(8) Online Reviewer. (Companies pay you to post reviews of a product or service)

(9) Flavorist. (test natural or artificial flavors for perfumes, food additives)

(10) Submarine Cook.*

(11) Legal Hacker.* (Companies pay you to security test new software)

*you can make a six-figure income a year at these jobs.

Don't forget to dress for success. Remember, it's every bit as much the gift of GARB as it is the gift of GAB, that will help land you the job of your dreams. (See SHOP)

Jump

...into a pool. with a rope. On a trampoline. Out of a plane (don't forget the chute). Jump for joy. Jump for all the jingle it's worth. It's like temporarily defying gravity...if just for a little while.

K

Keepsakes

Beautiful treasures representing people, places and times in our lives, keepsakes are what keep those memories alive in our hearts, and give us a very special kind of jingle. Each time we pick up a favorite picture, an antique vase, torn concert tickets or a treasured piece of family jewelry, we are reminded of those people and celebrations that helped mold us into who we are.

I have my grandmother's hand-carved secretary desk in my living room. Upon going through several boxes of pictures my dad passed on to me, I was thrilled to run across a PICTURE of my grandmother sitting at the desk writing Christmas cards, and my granddad had perfectly captured the moment. I immediately framed it and put it on the top shelf. There's not one day I don't walk by that desk and look at it, and transport myself back in time to her, her laughter and love of life, and the inspiring impact she had on mine.

I don't use them, I don't play golf, but I have my dad's treasured set of golf clubs in my front closet. They gave him so much joy; maybe one day I will be able to find the right person to give them to. But NOT YET!

The value of a keepsake is determined not by its dollar value, but by its "dear value." One of my most prized possessions is a little ceramic vase in the shape of a donkey pulling an open cart. At one time it was full of beautiful carnations and roses my dad took to the hospital to give my mom when I was born.

A plastic glazed Mother's Day plate with three sunflowers on it drawn in crayon with the words "I Love You" created by my then 7-year-old daughter Sarah stands in front of all the antique teacups and crystal in my curio cabinet.

In my living room sits a beautiful ceramic Lladro of a young woman sitting on a bench in a garden holding her hat by her side as she gazes at a baby bird sitting on the edge. My mom bought it in Spain, and carried that tiny crate first through the streets of Madrid, then customs, and then in her carry-on bag through three airport terminals to get it home to give to me. I knew it was expensive, but what mattered to me is that it reminded her of me, and that she went through all this to get it for me.

Kids

Whether you have children or not, you know people who do. And I don't think any of us can say that kids don't add jingle to our lives (sometimes the ring is a little discordant, but nevertheless a jingle!) Kids say---and do---the darndest things. Children can give an unparalleled perspective on life untainted by prejudice or life experience. Like a blank painter's canvas on which they can write their own impressions of life instead of viewing the ones made by others. And for those of us who are parents, our kids will always be our kids...no matter how old they get.

Speaking first as a child, my mother and I fought only over hair, makeup and skirt length. But those fights were doozies. She went so far one day as to put my pasty-colored trend makeup on herself and say, "See? You're chalk white! Do you want to be mistaken for a GHOST? You need COLOR!!" And I loved my mom dearly, but she did make attempts from time to time (as all mothers do) to sell me a ticket on numerous guilt trips. Like, "That's ok, if you don't have time to come over for the dinner I took FOUR HOURS to make because you'd PREFER to go to a concert. I mean, The Eagles WILL be back in another three YEARS. But THAT'S OK." Once I left for college, and got a reality check on just how lucky I was to have the family I had, I called her a month after getting there and simply said, "You were right." Mom answered, "About what?" I said, "Everything." I heard first a gasp and then dead air. "Mom?" I said. "Yes. I am just sitting pinching myself to be sure I just heard what you said." Dad told me later that she was literally jingling around the house for the rest of the day, and pretty much the rest of the YEAR.

Dad and I were very close; I guess you could say that I was the Ray family princess. But I didn't get my way on everything. Back then, you had to actually EARN your allowance and clean your room. The only time he ever got really mad at me was when I came to him one time and asked for a new bike, and he said, "Did you ask your mother?" "Of course," I answered, in a vain effort to convince him that I had her approval...when I hadn't. I made that mistake just one time. I had plenty of time to think about the consequences of doing it a second time during my two weeks of being grounded. But for all of his extensive education and high-level management position at his company, he was the funniest, down-to-earth, REAL person you could ever meet. I called Dad's response to work recognition the "aw, shucks" mentality.

From childhood on, he had to work for everything he had, and he passed that work ethic down to me. Dad was the epitome of the southern gentleman from top to toe. When he retired, he had the largest party on record at that time at Phillips. People from all over the company, from the mail room to the board room, came to wish him well. I know why.

My daughter Sarah gave me jingle MOST of the time. Except when she had her first slumber party at our house. Everything was going very well until she---and her seven little partners in crime, her friends---decided that they wanted to make ice cream sundaes about 2 a.m. Which would have been fine except that when they ran out of room in the kitchen, they took the party (plus five cartons of ice cream, three flavors of syrup and cones) into the CARPETED living room.) And then two of the kids wanted ice cream FLOATS, so bottles of coke and 7-up followed behind. They managed to do all this quietly. (Or maybe I was so tired that I slept through it) And then went to BED after wreaking this havoc. When I woke up and went out to the kitchen to put on my morning coffee, I couldn't GET to the coffee. All four kitchen countertops and floor -- PLUS the dining room table and floor -- were covered with soupy piles of ice cream, spilled soda and broken cones. It was like walking on flypaper; when you stepped down, you didn't step up. You were anchored to the floor with a shoe full of sticky mess. It was like a Braum's employee uprising gone bad. Plus, the kids ATE their creations on their sleeping bags, so the gook was all over their bedding too. I made the kids get up, and start cleaning up. It took until 8:30 to even make a dent in it. I went and picked up donuts for breakfast, because there wasn't room to cook breakfast. When the parents showed up at 9:30, the kids couldn't wait to leave. And I couldn't wait to get them out of there.

I had many proud moments with her. She never gave up on anything she decided she wanted to do, made great grades, loved animals and people, and was active in sports. Watching her take first place in a number of track meets and soccer games gave me so much jingle as a mother, but even more so because I knew it gave HER jingle.

Kiss

The kiss. One of life's most jingle-izing experiences. Go ahead, plant one...on your spouse, your child, your sibling, a good friend. The kiss expresses friendship, love, respect, peace or good luck. Or all of the above! And It definitely conveys jingle! Beyond the fact it makes people happy, it's also a documented fact that kissing people you care about at least once a day---or being kissed yourself---increases your life expectancy by at least five years. It can also boost your immune system, burn calories, improve allergies, benefit your heart, and even stop headaches!! So pucker up and peck your favorite foreheads, lips, and cheeks; a kiss tells the people you care about how much you DO. So, do it often. Make some "KISS-tory! "You'll jingle every day. And, don't forget to give your pets a hug and peck too. They love you unconditionally every day.

Kites

And no, I don't mean TELLING someone to go fly one, however tempting that may be. Go and REALLY fly one. They can be any size, any shape, cardboard, plastic, wood. And no, drones don't count.

No matter what shape it is, whether you make it, buy it or borrow it, get one and go find a big open space on a good windy day to give it wings. And take a bunch of kids with you.

Please refrain from flying one that's been painted to look like an American eagle. Or you may, like one of my neighbors and his son, encounter a real one looking for a mate. And you'll be running for a very, very long time.

L

Laugh

Laughter is not only truly the best medicine...it's CON-TAGIOUS! Just the act of doing it will make your whole body jingle. And laughter is one thing NO ONE will mind catching from you. Find something humorous in every day, and laugh about it. Even if you've had a day like Murphy's law on steroids, laughing will release tension, and make you much better able to deal with it. Of course, unless you're standing in front of a firing squad.

The mother of a family friend credits her recovery from cancer to the power of laughter. She would leave a chemotherapy session and head home to turn on the RTV channel. For hours, she would watch reruns of I Love Lucy, Bewitched, Red Skelton, The Carol Burnett Show, The Three Stooges, any Bob Hope or Doris Day movie plus anything else that made her laugh. The laughter was the lifter...of her spirits and her body's desire to get better. She became positive in spite of herself. So...JEST do it! Laugh!

Learn A New Language

Yes, learning a foreign language can give you a special kind of jingle: I call it POWER. When I went to Europe for a convention several years ago, I was the ONLY person in a group of 130 people who could speak French. And because of that, I was also the most popular! Yes, for seven magical days, I was the Pied Piper of Lausanne, Switzerland, leading an anxious group of American tourists all through the city streets. After all, I knew how to ask DIRECTIONS. Think of what this knowledge can do for you, during and AFTER your trip:

1. You know how to ask where all the most important things are: (bathroom, restaurants, train station, trendy shops, and yes, McDonald's. And the American Embassy if you do something stupid.)

2. You don't have to call the front desk at your hotel to ask what a bidet is.

3. You can make better deals with the local gift shop owners, because you know what the price REALLY is.

4. If you pretend like you're struggling with the language as you nervously scan your *French For Dummies* dictionary for the right words, the locals will often feel sorry for you and give you even a better deal. (My dad did this in Paris; but he really WAS struggling; he was in a perfume shop buying a gift for Mom, and the clerks were so impressed by his efforts, that they put together a samples basket of 30 pricey perfumes and gave it to him as a bonus gift. Mom not only got her Chanel #5, she got a fragrance for every day of the month). He did know how to say "Merci."

5. You just sound cool.

6. When you're back home, you can say what you really think to family, friends, and your employer, and they won't have a clue. Oh, and be sure to SMILE while you're doing it.

7. You can put "bi-lingual" on your resume.

8. Threaten your misbehaving kids half in English, half in the foreign language, while wildly waving your hands. They'll do what you want every time. Either because they believe you or they think you're crazy, and they're not taking a chance either way.

9. You can read the subtitles on foreign films.

10. You can read the menu at that great restaurant. You'll impress your friends, and also ensure you don't get smoked squid instead of Chicken Marengo.

The most fun I had was at a local clock shop. The owner and I verbally sparred for about 15 minutes in very fast French, until I finally could not keep up with the speed of his speech. He suddenly started speaking in perfect English, and told me he had attended college in the States. He was testing me to see how far I could take the language. He told me if I could stay in the country for at least another 2-3 weeks, I would start THINKING in French. I already was. For my efforts, he gave me a great deal on gifts to take home too!!

Love

Love...A very small word for a very big emotion. Love may not make the world go around, but it sure makes the ride a whole lot better. Love is what makes the great times great, and the bad times easier to get through. And there are as many different kinds of love as there are people to express them. The love of a parent for a child. The love between good friends. And what has been the motivation for poets, songwriters and authors for over twenty centuries...romantic love. For the sake of winning the heart of another, wars have been fought, people have lied, stolen, sacrificed their all for a chance at love. And there is a difference between loving someone and "being in love" with someone. You can love a lot of people in your life; but if you're lucky, you will experience the "in-love" feeling with only a very few, and ideally, one incredible person. Remember, it takes only three seconds to say "I love you," three hours to explain it, and a lifetime to prove it. TRUE love lasts during the good times, the bad times, and for ALL time.

M

Macy's Thanksgiving Day Parade

Long celebrated as the official kickoff to the Christmas holiday season, go or at least watch this American classic event. I have attended one in my lifetime. It's amazing. Every year, the parade features more and more balloons, floats, entertainment and just good fun. The jingle is evident in the faces of the bundled up people of every age along the parade route. It's a favorite Thanksgiving tradition at my house, between the breakfast casserole and the official Thanksgiving food fest.

Marriage

To keep the monotony out of monogamy, and keep that jingle in your marriage, you need to practice the three C's: Communication, Caring and Compromise. Without these three C's, you might be looking at the big D down the road. Be transparent in all things, especially romance and finance. Guys, want to get your marriage off to a great start? Make a great marriage PROPOSAL!

My husband schemed with a local restaurant to present me with a very original invitation to the altar state. He made a reservation at our favorite Italian restaurant on a weeknight (not a weekend, so I wouldn't suspect), and had me come straight from work to meet him there. He was waiting at the bar when I came in, and we were seated at a quiet table in the back. He made sure that MY back was to the rest of the patrons. While it was a full house, we seemed to have exceptionally good service that evening, and I do mean exceptional. As in refilling my water glass every five minutes.

After dinner, he left the table---supposedly to go to the men's room---and then returned. Suddenly, the waiter appeared with what I just KNEW was a ring box and set it down in front of me. Excited, I was certain what the contents had to be; but he didn't say a word, and just suggested I open it. My trembling hands opened the lid, only to discover what appeared to be a very cheap watch inside. Terribly disappointed, but struggling to be polite, I hesitated a moment, and said thank you. Then he smiled and said, "Look at the watch." I did. It was running. "What time does it say?" I said, "7:30." "What date does it say?" I said," December 17th." And then he said, "I wanted you to know the exact day and time I asked you to marry me." I was so stunned, I was speechless. Too speechless to even answer.

So this dear man was on his knees already, with the whole room poised to **hear** that answer. He got that "uh-oh"- I- am-about to experience- public- humiliation- be-cause- she's- going- to- say- no" look on his face, and had to ask me again: "so...WILL you?" I finally got off my cloud, floated back down to earth and said yes; then, the waiter brought the REAL box with the REAL ring in it (plus a red rose) to give him to put on my finger. When he supposedly had gone to the men's room, he had gone to the bar instead, got the watch, set it, wrapped it, and locked in the date and time to coincide with when he would have the waiter bring it to me.

This was a "gotcha" beyond all gotchas. I got a lot of "softs" that evening: soft music, soft candlelight, but I got what I really wanted: a ROCK. And yes, he certainly "rocked" MY world that day. It was Love IN the rocks, because it was an absolutely beautiful ring. I consider myself the superwoman of surprises, but this was the best one I had ever had. Helzberg Diamonds has our story on their website. I named our story "A 'Timely' Question." Thank you, Mike Brosky, for your help.

We've been married 11 years, and look forward to many more. But if your marriage should end in divorce (sadly, 50% do), you can still get some jingle from writing a book about it. Some suggested titles:

Split and Sane

Split Decision

Desperate Spouse Lies

A Good Man...The Cure For the Common Ex

On the 12th of Never...A Guide to Ex-Spouse Communication

Re-Altar State: Second Time Is Better

On The Date Again...Guide for the Savvy Single

Your Wish Was Not My Command

Your Cheating Heart Did Tell On---And Cost---You

Medical

Can't figure out why a trip to the doctor or pharmacy could be full of jingle? Oh, but it can be, even if you just listen to what OTHER people say there. Here's one prescription for jingle. One day I was at my local Walgreen's, where a customer had just stepped up to the "Consultation" window with a question. The pharmacist said, "Yes, ma'am, how can I help you?" The customer answered, "Are there any side effects for this medication...apart from bankruptcy?" Then, I remember overhearing a woman who was in to pick up prescriptions to take prior to a medical test. Upon being handed several bottles, along with an enema kit, she gave the pharmacist a shocked look and said, "When the doctor said he was getting me prepared for a GI Series, I thought I was coming in to see you because you were the guy who scalped some tickets to get me into a soldier's-only baseball game." Oh, I can't ever forget the guy in the hospital bed next to my friend I was visiting. He was saying to the nurse that he thought postoperative care meant that his mailman was coming to see him.

Money

Money can't buy you happiness, but it can make a pretty good down payment. Yes, having literal jingle in your pocket---and your bank account---can make life a lot better, as long as that money is your servant and not your master. The stock market always keeps people buzzing. If you're not careful, those blue chip stocks can turn into cow chips overnight! A friend of mine called me with concerns about information she had just received from her stockbroker that she wanted me to clarify, which I was happy to do!

Merrill Lynch - What you'd LIKE to do to Merrill

Broker Year - What we are this year as compared to last year

Capital Gains - Congress getting another raise

Day Trader - Ebay Junkie

Prime Rate - what a good steak costs

Market Turnaround - return trip to grocery store for forgotten milk

Bull Market - a bar filled with salespeople in ANY field

Music

Whether you jive to it, drive to it, dance or romance to it, music is the soundtrack of our lives. From country to classical, rock to jazz, gospel to rap, music adds jingle to our lives. What's so great about music is that with the pop-in of a CD on your boombox or a download of an MP3 to your computer, you can pick the music to match our mood....or IMPROVE IT! Kind of like you choose a cologne. And you can change it anytime you want! I start my day with a Dash of disco, attack my inbox with Abba, drive home with the Eagles, and have a little bubbly with Michael Buble at home.

Or you can MAKE the music YOURSELF.

I actually AM a musician---a "closet" pianist. I only come out of it to play for myself and for special people in my life. You might say I got a "Handel" on my life at six, and studied until age fifteen, when I decided I did not want the life of a concert pianist. But I took away so much more from that experience than a specific skill level of piano playing.

My teacher, Martha Boucher, was a major inspiration to me well beyond my years spent sitting at a Steinway keyboard. Holding a Ph.D in Music and a Juilliard graduate, she had a passion for music, and an equal passion to share it with others. I learned several things: If you do what you love, you'll be rich in life, regardless of the size of the paycheck. I also learned about discipline, hard work and pride in a job well done. There is now a Martha M. Boucher scholarship offered by OU. No surprise there.

But, oh, did I hate music theory class, because it was math! Aargh! I felt like I was back in English class, except this time I was learning to read and diagram a bunch of black circles with funny-looking lines hanging from them called NOTES! Quarter, half, eighth and sixteenths, with and without dots and funny names under them like legato, allegretto, allegro and glissando. But she always gave out the most original achievement gifts to her students: cool music pins, statuettes, ribbons, piano models. You just wanted to do your best for her! Grieg's Piano Concerto #9 was my final accomplishment. (I got through it ONCE after two months of practice.) Then, I was done.

So now I get my jingle representing OTHERS with those musical gifts who do play. Joesf Glaude, the jazz musician I represent, plays all over Tulsa, the state and the country with an engaging and entertaining variety of jazz, pop jazz, and blues. He and his band, Guitars Gone Wild, give away as much income as they make in bookings to a number of worthy causes in the city, benefitting charities that support the homeless, veterans, children, and the arts. He even wrote---and donated---a song to Soldier's Wish.

I have also enjoyed representing Jimmy Henley, acclaimed banjo virtuoso who first appeared on the popular, 70's TV show *Hee Haw* as a teen, and then later made his musical stamp in bluegrass over the years, touring all across America and around the world with iconic entertainer and music legend Roy Clark. Jimmy has taken the stage to benefit a number of charities, including Soldier's Wish, plus entertaining at a number of public and private events. He made his *New Directions* national debut with the Bartlesville Symphony, my hometown. Now, that was some serious jingle!

N

National Science Foundation

If you don't already know about this government entity, the NSF is the non-medical research organization who has come up with "creative" ways to spend our taxpayer dollars through its federal grant programs over the last many years. I guess I get my jingle because of how ridiculous some of them are: (otherwise I'd get really mad).

1. How long shrimp can run on a treadmill.

2. How playing on Facebook's Farmville can help people make and keep friends.

3. How quickly parents respond to trendy baby names.

4. Why the same basketball teams always dominate March Madness.

They fund approximately 10,000 of the 50,000 grant requests they get each year. Their budget is approximately $7 billion per year.

Network

Connecting people together successfully for their mutual benefit, just for the sheer joy of it, and expecting nothing in return, is a real "jingle"-ation. I have so many stories of my own, and I jingle every time I think of them. Here are a few.

I connected a model looking for a part in a music video to a country music singer who was making one. The singer wound up on *America's Got Talent*; the model now models in top shows around the country. Loni and Bailey became great friends, and have helped one another's professional careers. And a totally unexpected jingle for me came as a result; I got to meet legendary entertainer Tony Orlando, as he was a family friend of the girls' moms. (Thank you, Sandy!) A chance phone call from a music producer in Branson looking for a fill-in performer made possible a connection for an entertainer who was looking for that big break to start his career in Nashville.

I connected a veterans' charity called Soldier's Wish, who was looking to grant wishes of homes to deserving members of our military, to a new foundation (that AN-OTHER client had networked me to) who was looking to give them away!

I connected my main production agent and voiceover guru who, after producing several commercials for Soldier's Wish, called me one day and had decided he wanted to devote more of his time to help them succeed.

I connected a young woman restarting her life to someone I had just met only weeks before, who heads up a local municipal agency working with people just like her; She is being trained for a great job and a promising future; they even help with interviewing skills, resumes, and even dressing for success!

I connected a friend of mine---who wanted to donate HIS time to make wooden inspirational plaques to benefit a hospice---to my personal wood flooring company, who gave them more than they would ever need.

A dear friend of mine called me one day; their church was looking for someone to start up a praise and worship band; a musician client of mine had always dreamed of doing that for a church. People have called me the "Network Queen."

I don't need a tiara; I am just a Connector; I pay attention to things going on around me as I go through life, and when I see ways to connect people together for mutual benefit, I try to make it happen. We can ALL be connectors.

And, it works very much the other way. Be very grateful and heap all the jingle you can upon all the people who have connected YOU to jingle opportunities! Remember, it's not what you take with you that matters, it's what you LEAVE behind as a legacy.

New Year's Eve Party

It's the annual "sip, sip, hooray" event that brings in every New Year. But jingle in moderation, or you will be getting into bed with a severe hangover; or worse, getting in a police car for a trip to the local hoosegow if you drink and drive. My husband forgot to shut the back passenger door all the way while getting into the back seat of our friends' car. Our driver took a sharp turn to get on the freeway, the door swung out, and my husband found himself about to have a very close encounter with Highway 169 before we were able to grab him by his belt buckle and pull him in. He didn't even NEED coffee to help him wake up the next morning.

No

...Yes, "no" is a great way to say a big "YES" to more jingle...and sanity...in your life. You just need to know how and when to say it! How do you get jingle from saying no? Easy. As a younger woman, I was always being asked to be on this committee or that committee, to fill in for someone who was sick, to serve on this or that board, to volunteer at this or that event. CON-STANTLY. And here's what I found out: the more you do, the more you will be ASKED to do. I know this sounds terrible, but when I moved from my hometown church to a Tulsa church, I told NO ONE that I could play the piano, because I knew I would get a life sentence to do it on demand once I let the word out. Giving back and helping others is very important, but it's all about BALANCE. When you have no personal time to say yes to doing anything for yourself, you are "out of jingle." Be wise...PRIORITIZE! You will have a lot more jingle in your life if you do! A good rule of thumb is to give away 10% of your time and talent, just as you would give a check to your church. Hey, it's a contribution, the currency's just different! So, keep your life in the "sane lane;" Say yes to the NO!

O

Oklahoma

Ok, I have to brag a little on my home state. I have had over a half-century of jingle living here. Like the song, Oklahoma is thousands of square miles dotted by rolling hills, plains and bustling cities. But like any other state, certain idiosyncrasies distinguish us from other places. Below is a partial list:

It doesn't bother us to use an airport named after a man who died in a plane crash. (For your non-Okies, Will Rogers Airport)

We can properly pronounce "Eufaula, Gotebo, Okemah and Chickasha."

We think people who complain about the wind in their states are sissies.

We will choose a parking place five blocks away with shade over one without it only ten feet from the door.

Our "place at the lake" has wheels under it.

We know that everything goes better with Ranch.

We can tell you how many bales of hay our car will hold.

We have used the words "fixin to" at least five times a year.

We have the only state where we can go from wearing shorts to a parka in the same week. (And sometimes in the same DAY).

But it's certainly my "state of mind,"---and heart---and I love being an "Okie."

Older (As In "Getting")

Who says you can't jingle about getting older? I know I'd much prefer that to the alternative. And what choice do we have? am frankly over fifty, and one of the ways I know I'm getting older is the effect ANY medication has on me. One-half of the smallest dose of an "as-needed" anxiety medication is enough to make me so relaxed I would thank a dentist for giving me a root canal, or laugh at a whole baseball team who just tracked mud through my house. (I did both.) A whole pill would put me in a coma for two days. Just think of it. If I needed heart surgery, I could just hear the doctor---who had heard this about me---saying, "Oh, just give her a little IV Valium and a local, and we're good to go." It would certainly reduce my anesthesia expense, but would also certainly raise the (still conscious) patient participation level in the operating room right after the first "#3 scalpel please, nurse."

More ways you know you're getting older:

1. Your love life has gone from passion to COM-passion.

2. Your back goes out more than you do.

3. When you hear the word Hardware, you only think of screen door hooks and hinges.

4. You feel like the "morning after," but you didn't go anywhere last night.

5. You're wise enough to watch your step, but too old to walk anywhere.

6. You set your watch alarm to 30 minutes before Golden Corral's senior buffet opens.

7. Your knee can predict the next rainstorm.

8. Your teeth don't sleep in the same room that you do.

9. Your monthly hair "brightening" bill is more than your car payment.

10. You like to rock to music...in a chair on the porch.

My age has given me a brand new identity: I am now Wonder Woman. I wonder where my keys are, where my cell phone went and where my money is. Somebody has definitely made a withdrawal from my memory bank. One time I came in the house and set my keys and debit card in the fridge and left my groceries sitting on the counter. Talk about cold cash and warm ice cream.

Out of the Box Thinking

Get out of your rut! Doing the same thing the same way every day will NOT help you get your jingle on! You know, it's hard to see the label on a bottle when you're sitting inside of it. Sometimes you just need to step back, get outside of your current surroundings, and make some new decisions based on new thinking. But always be sure the different thing is the RIGHT thing. As Mark Twain said, "Always do right. That will gratify some of the people, and astonish the rest."

P

Park It.

Anywhere. In your neighborhood, close to your office, around the corner from your school. Walk, bike or skateboard your way to that jingle only intermingling with nature can give you. If you don't have one close by, create your own oasis in your backyard. (See "Walk.") It's the perfect getaway from the real world, if only for a little while.

Party

Being a carefree guest at a great party is a great jingle-izer! You don't have to cook, clean or come up with entertainment...all you have to do is show up.

A few suggestions, however, on how to mingle and make conversation, the science of "guesthood." If you don't know the host very well, a trip to their medicine cabinet shortly after your arrival could give you some clues (It also could get you an abrupt invitation to leave as well, so be discreet). Then you can say brilliant things like:

1. The creme hair dyes really do last longer, don't they, Betty?

2. Just love that Super Poligrip denture adhesive. It would be pretty risky to put out a carrots and celery appetizer tray otherwise, wouldn't it, Carol?

3. Having three kids in school can really be stressful, can't it, Mary?

4. My hemorrhoids are really acting up today. Linda, can I borrow your donut pillow for the evening?

You can introduce your CLOTHES to your host. "Nancy, here are my Nine West Shoes." (like the shoes are going to respond.) And I know you would be SO interested in seeing my Vera Wang dress; I got it on sale. Oh, you have a Michael Kors purse TOO! And in RED!

If you really like the party favor your host gives you as you prepare to leave, please don't ask how much it is and where he or she bought it. And don't ask for a "to go" gift to take home to your spouse and/or kids.

Pay It Forward

Anytime and any way you can. At the grocer, cleaners, fast-food restaurant. At the drive-through, I like to call it "drive-through donating." ...towards a more jingle-filled day for someone ELSE. One guy I know paid for 20 Big Macs and supersized fries, the post-game meal for a van full of 12-year-old athletes ahead of him whose team had just lost their regional soccer championship. It was obvious by their sad faces hanging out the window that the sign "Take State" should have read "Didn't Take State," so this caring man made their day a winner in spite of it.

A former radio client of mine owns a successful office furniture store. He has a big event every year called a "Chair"-ity. He always hosts it during the Christmas holidays, which is also a time he knows that businesses need to spend any extra money they have in their budgets for office equipment or supplies to be able to take the tax writeoff for the year. So he discounts every chair in the store, and gives the proceeds to the John 3:16 Mission for the homeless.

I had an interesting experience in paying it forward. Frankly, I wasn't sure whether or not I should put it under this heading or under "Gift." A prospective client I had met a few months earlier had told me they would get back with me when they were ready to launch their company. Four months later, I get an enthusiastic call (I still have the voicemail) that said they were ready to go, and wanted to meet me the next week to get all the media booked and to start production. I was excited as I drove to the meeting on Monday. I had scheduled 1-1/2 hours for the meeting plus travel time, so I felt like it was ok to schedule a conference call with another client 2-1/2 hours later that morning.

We go over all the ideas and concepts, and everything seems to be going well. As I saw the hands on the restaurant clock inching closer and closer to the time I had to leave, I noticed the couple seemed at a loss for words and looking nervous. They finally said that they had no gas money to get back to their office, and wanted to borrow money from me.

Wow. Let's review. They don't call me for four months, and then call me to hire me for a huge project that will cost thousands of dollars to implement. And then they want me to give THEM money because THEY'VE had financial problems. I was speechless. Part of me wanted to just get up and leave at their complete lack of professionalism; I felt like I was being used. But then, I re-membered that someone had once bought me gas during a difficult time, and maybe this was MY chance to pay it forward.

But I was fast running out of time. I don't carry much cash with me, and I told them they would have to follow me (in their late model upscale sedan) to a Quik Trip close to my office, and that we had to leave NOW. We did, and they truly had NO GAS in their car. I know be-cause I filled their whole tank up for them. I have no idea how they planned to get home if I had not helped them out. The jury is out as of this writing whether or not I will offer to work with them. I had a couple of calls later on meetings they were going to have with other partners, but nothing since.

Pigeon Race

If you've never seen one of these fly-fests, you must go! I've gone to three presented as charity fundraisers. Each race pigeon is tagged with a name and number; you pick your feathered contender on arrival, and they are released from a special "launch" platform at a specific time at the event venue. When they take off, it's like watching a giant screeching white sheet with wings. A "webcam" is put into place at the finish line (their home, several miles away) and a wide-screen computer allows you to watch them on their journey. You can imagine; these birds pass over a lot of highway traffic on their way. I can just hear their race conversation now: "So many windshields, so little time." But it's "Fowl Play" at its finest!

Purpose

Nothing gives jingle like having purpose in your life. It's a reason you get up every day. According to Mark Twain, the two most important days in a person's life are (1) when they were born, and (2) when they realize WHY they were born. Sometimes we have to put a lot of keys in a lot of life opportunity doors before the right one opens. Don't be afraid; take a chance. I had a college friend who said he felt that his only purpose in life was to serve as a warning to others. He did become happy and successful later...a little later than those of us WITHOUT this attitude. Hey, if you don't think anyone cares about you, just try missing a couple of car payments. In your effort to meet more people, don't get desperate enough to EVER put up a sign outside your home that says "Solicitors Wanted." Remember, some days you are the bug, some days you are the windshield. It all evens out.

Q

Queen

For all the ladies reading this book, jingle knowing that you are the queen of your life, and that you deserve all the royal things that life has to offer you. When life hands you problems, just adjust your tiara, straighten your train and move on! Right, Skarlett? Always leave a trail of sparkle wherever you go! Preface your signature on your checks with "Her Majesty." Always refer to your car or truck as the "coach" when handing the keys to the restaurant valet. And you must perfect the Queen's "wave." You know, when you hold your right hand straight up in the air and twist it back and forth as if you are unscrewing a really high light bulb. However, you will get stares if you do this at your daughter's soccer match. Post a car window hanger that says, "Queen on Board."

R

Radio

Who can't get some jingle listening to the radio? You can literally "dial on demand" to hear whatever you want. But the DJs are who make the shows what they are. It's like having a good friend who sits and talks with you as you drink your coffee, decide what to wear, and put out the dog. And never needs to know who you are or needs a response (well, unless you want to be Caller #6 to win some free pizza or sports tickets). The *morning* show DJs are particularly entertaining. After all, since they're been up since 4 a.m., what comes out of their mouths can really jingle up your morning.

My most favorite all-time radio personality was Billy Parker, who just retired from Scripps this past year. Anybody from Tulsa, or anyone who knows anything about country music, knows the name Billy Parker. His radio and music career spanned five decades, his final gig being his wildly popular Saturday morning show on Big Country 99.5 Radio, *Billy Parker's Country Junction*. Several of my clients were on his show over the years. It was a "Jingle"-fest of fun in his studio every time we went up there. The diversity of guests ranged from bullriders to banjo players, shriners to singers, and everything in between. On and off-air, Billy was the funniest, talented and most gracious person I have ever met in the business. They had to give him TWO retirement parties, his "Thanks A Lot" tribute party at the Cain's Ballroom, and then a station retirement party.

Anyone who knows me knows that I have worked for a few radio stations in my time. And loved it. One station I worked for had an on-air Sunday stint available for a few hours due to the regular DJ's recent leg operation, and my then-boyfriend-not-yet-husband Bob had the perfect voice for the job. But he had never done radio before, and because he had a full-time job in a totally different field, he needed to convince them somehow to try him out. Considering he had absolutely no industry experience or "demo tape," we had to get REALLY creative. The station was an "oldies" format, so I sat down one night to write this for him:

TOP TEN REASONS I QUALIFY TO DJ ON KOOL 106:

1. I don't have to Google the net to know who the "Fab Four" are.

2. I know Mick Jagger's therapist.

3. I know that "KC and the Sunshine Band" is not the weather team from a Missouri TV station.

4. I can make the station extra revenue by endorsing Depends, Dentu-Creme and Preparation H.

5. I will only hang up on contest callers who think "Woodstock" is fence material on sale at Lowe's.

6. I'll fix your CEO's private airplane for free if you get me tickets to "1964."

7. I have nine year's experience in the U.S. AIR Force.

8. I know the Supremes are NOT a pizza chain.

9. I have a great radio face.

10. I know just how to say "thank you, thank you very much."

He didn't get the DJ job, but they DID hire him to do voice work!

RV

Owning one of these can really give you lots of jingle. The freedom of taking one of these four-wheeled fortresses out on the open road to travel the American landscape can certainly beckon you. Think for a second about owning one of these before you go out and actually buy one, however. First, you have to change your entire vocabulary. When hubby wants to go to the store, he says, "I'll be taking the HOUSE out for a couple of hours; need anything?" The postman will also find it hard to reach you, especially when your address is Exit 56 off Interstate 60, then exit 57, then exit 58…

A friend of mine owns one, and said having a flat tire was the longest time they ever spent in one place. And good luck getting a cup of sugar from a neighbor, unless you're camped in a QT parking lot, or the Food Channel is on a road trip. And dinner out is whatever the blue plate special is at the nearest truck stop.

Respect

Respect yourself...and others. Always seek respect over attention; it lasts longer. Respect your spouse. Respect those with opinions that differ from yours. Respect our country's flag. Respect your parents. Respect those in authority. We'll all be a lot more jingle-filled if we do.

Retirement

Aaah, retirement. The laid-back, stress-free future we all look forward to as the jingle-filled culmination of our working careers. To keep your retirement golden, remember that you are only leaving behind one part of your life; you are starting a NEW chapter. You are not retiring from LIFE. So don't trade in your office chair for the recliner and the TV remote. You won't last long. I have one friend who owned a brick and mortar business he drove to every day for 25 years. Holding a computer degree, he never had time to spend with his favorite hobby: website development. He spent only a few thousand dollars to add an extra room to his home, and now builds websites and does computer repairs for friends and family. And can work in his PJs! (Well, until he has to deliver it to the customer).

One of my most favorite people is my family banker. By the time you read this book, he will have retired. He was, and is still, greatly missed by all of his co-workers and customers. In fact, I wrote a top ten list of the conditions under which we, his customers and co-workers, would ALLOW him to retire. So, here goes:

OK, Stephen, you can retire IF:

1. You buy a Caribbean island and give us free tickets to come visit you.

2. You buy any island and give us free tickets to come visit you.

3. You buy a condo, ranch, house, beach cabana, villa, log cabin or really big tent and give us free tickets to come visit you.

4. You return to Bartlesville every quarter to take each of us out to lunch INDIVIDUALLY and get all our life updates.

5. If you don't buy an island, you throw us a barbeque once a month at your home, to include two hours of free "Colaw's Cashflow Counseling."

6. You set up a Facebook "Colaw Community" group page for only your customers, and give us weekly hot money management tips.

7. You remember all our birthdays...including cake.

8. You give each of us a year's supply of Kleenex, because we will be crying over your departure for at least that long.

9. You get us an Arvest trust customer group discount to a psychiatrist, because we will all need treatment for "separation anxiety syndrome" once you leave.

10. You agree to return in one year if your customers decide they just can't make it without you. (which will be everyone.)

Ride

Take a ride! ...on a roller coaster. A ferris wheel. The Mad Hatter teacups at Disney World. It's worth it. It fills the bill for thrills WITHOUT the bill for gas or insurance! However, you may need chill PILLS to have the courage to board one in the first place. An additional word of caution...have that chili dog with cheese with the cotton candy chaser AFTER you get off.

Roll Down A Grassy Hill

For all the freedom and jingle it gives, just do it and revel in the fun. And if you live in Tulsa, just be sure the hill you choose doesn't run into Interstate 44. (it's one of the most popular, thereby one of the most dangerous). This does not end well. And don't do this if you tend to have dizzy spells or have just been to Ben's Beer Bistro. In the wintertime, use a sled with GPS!

S

Sale

No matter if it's a half price, holiday, after-whatever-holiday sale, moving or remodeling sale, ANY sale is a real jingle journey for ME. From the parking aisles to the shopping aisles, it's a trip ALWAYS worth taking. And whether you need the item(s) or not is irrelevant. It's the thrill of the conquest over paying full price on ANYTHING! It's like scaling Everest, one receipt at a time. And climate-controlled too.

Shopping

Hey, it doesn't ring everyone's jingle bell, but it does MINE. If you don't like to shop for yourself, shop for OTHERS. After all, everyone needs SOMETHING. Retail therapy is my go-to cure for lots of things! Unless the reason I'm depressed is because I did too MUCH of it. Then I just take a CANDY-depressant; that works every time. I don't have to have a mission; and often, when I do, I don't find what I went for, and bring home three bags of something else. But never go shopping with your spouse; that's like going hunting in the forest with the game warden. You never get what you want. And if you buy it anyway, you'll going to get penalized!

And always be in shape for shopping. Be sure to do some deep knee bends so you can reach those elusive bottom shelves where they hide all the best bargains they don't want you to find. And practice some wind sprints so you can make car trips faster to unload your treasures and still get back in before the "doorbuster" sale is over. Stretch yourself; and your credit cards, to max shopping status!

If the store is having a remodeling sale, let their dust become your deals! (Hey, it's less stuff they have to move back.)

And don't fight people for items; just distract them to other aisles. Throw your voice and say, " Buy one, get THREE pairs of shoes FREE!" Or even better, "Free Chocolate at Register 6!"

Remember, the best things in life...eventually go ON SALE!

That's when you go shopping to pay your husband back for booking a camping trip instead of the cruise YOU wanted for this year's summer vacation.

Sing

In the shower. In the car. To a baby. For a group of seniors at a retirement community. In your church choir or praise band. Regardless of your skill level, singing simply means elongated speech, a melodic way of speaking your heart and your mind. From praising to punk, romantic to rap, it's a great way to get and give jingle...both to yourself and others.

Stein Mart

My personal shopping paradise, these two words should be in the dictionary under Fabulous Fashion! This store needs to be a state all its own. I know it's MY awesome apparel address. You've heard about R and R, well, it's called R.S.R. for me. (Rita's Second Residence). I love this store. It's name may be Stein Mart, but to me it's Mine Mart. My car GPS ("Yvonne") is pre-set for 91st and Memorial. And if I have the incredibly poor judgment to drive past that beckoning green sign, Yvonne starts yelling at me to "go back, go back!" And the car starts shaking. I yield; I stop. I shop. Once I leave the store, if the "trunk load" monitor is not registering at least four outfits (or at least two purses and/or one pair of shoes), my "Spend--ometer" light comes on, indicating that I am low on fashion, and need to return to work out that credit card more. So back through the doors I go. I will never hear "Go Glam or Go Home," because I (or at least my clothes) will always look jingle-perfect wherever I go. Without wiping out my wallet.

Stein Mart is the place where I bought the Christmas Jingle pin that inspired me to write these books, and gave me a whole new outlook on life. Hey, between Red Dot Sales, Blue Slash Sales and 14-Hour Sales, you can shop by NUMBER---AND COLOR---every day! Oh, and don't forget THE BIG SALE. I'm sure that if famous American humorist Will Rogers was here today, and had visited Stein Mart, he would just have to add to his famous quote that he never met a man OR a PRICE TAG he didn't like. (I certainly haven't!) If I miss even a week, I deal with S.M. S.A.S. (Stein Mart Separation Anxiety Syndrome). It's my Mecca, my oasis, my clothes encounter of the best kind! And for the special ladies facing some financial challenges I also buy for, the savings translate into more great stuff I can buy to help facilitate their life success and positive self-image. If I can ever fight my way out of women's apparel---AND still have room in my cart---Stein Mart has great buys on menswear and home decor too.

Surprise

Surprises are a wonderful way to give unexpected jingle to people you care about. Surprise someone for a birthday, anniversary, a homecoming, or for no reason at all. It's not about the gift you present, it's your presence with the gift. "No-reason" surprises are the absolute best, because it shows that you consider every day with them a special occasion, a reason to celebrate their presence in your life. Do not surprise ANYONE with a new pet, however. Especially at Christmas. Think about it. The recipient will have to potty train this new furry friend during the WINTER. And like what happened to me when I made this mistake several years ago, I found out upon the delivery of a new Lab puppy to their home that my friend's husband was ALLERGIC to dogs. After one sniff, his cheeks were redder than Santa's cheeks after sitting too long on a housetop with a broken chimney on Christmas Eve. We all got to celebrate Christmas Day in the ER.

Going back in time to 2013, my husband surprised an entire elevator full---and later a deck full---of people on an anniversary cruise. He left our stateroom early to get coffee for me. Normal enough, right? What was different was what he was WEARING. While I was still snoozing away, he had donned his tuxedo shirt, black jacket and red bow tie and cumberbund, and was wearing it over a pair of white SHORTS. Add to this vision, tuxedo shoes with bright red sport socks. He completed the outfit with sunglasses and went strolling on the top deck with a martini, speaking to passengers in his best British accent. He just wanted to see what people would do. A third of the people thought he was drunk and forgot to take off his suit from the night before, another third just thought he was crazy, And one-third (the ones who were already on their third margarita) thought he fit right in. And I got pictures of it all (once I got up there). I called it the "shock walk." People were even stopping to take selfies with HIM. When asked his name, he would say in his best attempt at a British accent, "Brumm. Bob Brumm." And then stir his "martini."

T

Travel

Travel. It can be some of the best jingle you can do AWAY from home! But if you want to **keep** your jingle, be careful, not about where you go, but how you GET there without a stay in the local jail. These days, traveling ANYWHERE is jingle-challenging. Everyone jokes about the TSA; they do have a very hard job. But this story is priceless. My husband and I had just landed in Miami after a cruise with our dear friends Dennis and Sharon. I had forgotten to pack my portable electric hair rollers in my checked-on luggage; so, I had to put them in my carry-on bag. As soon as TSA saw their outline on the camera, I was abruptly pulled from the line and taken to a holding room. The curlers clearly had the brand name "Conair Hot Sticks" printed on them, but this woman---yes, a woman---was examining it as if it were the newest in demolition technology. Think about it; twenty 7" tall rubber sticks in a cylinder-shaped container with a cord wrapped around it. I saw curlers; they saw pink and purple -tinted C-4. My bra had metal underwire, so then I had to deal with that; and a 3-inch hairclip with a whopping 1/4" strip of metal set off the electronic policeman the third time. We almost missed our connecting flight to Tulsa. The same thing happened to me when we were returning from New York with four bottles of gourmet salad dressings in a gift box that I had purchased at Wegman's. On screen, they looked like a case of AK-47 gun clips.

My husband Bob almost got the chance to sign off on repairs so we could fly to Atlanta enroute to catching a cruise ship. The flight had already been delayed twice, and my spouse, the aircraft mechanic (for another airline) went up to ask what was going on. All of a sudden I saw him leaving with the ticket agent and heading onto the aircraft. The pilot reported that they had repairs done on a landing gear problem, but could not take off until a supervisor from said airline inspected and signed off, and no inspector was to be found. Bob presented his badge and said, "I'll do it." Since his airline's mechanics sometimes do repairs on other carriers while in Tulsa, he had the authority. They made a call, and it got done. When we got on the plane, we suddenly got upgraded to first class seats all the way to Atlanta and on to Miami!

TV Reality Shows

"Wars."

From Storage to Skin, from Window to Whales, Food to Fashion, everybody's fighting someone else to win money or fame with their projects, purchases or perseverance! And the rules are equally ridiculous.

Rescue/The Impossible.

From Bars to Hotels to Restaurants, these shows are the new Mission Impossible; they're just remodeling and renovating instead of shooting and spying. Industry experts, teams of designers, the newest technological inventions, chefs and financial advisors come in to turn these establishments' theme songs from "The Impossible Dream" into "Oh Happy Day."

Real Anything.

From Real Housewives of _____(insert city here, I'm sure there's a show for it), to "Really Stretching It" shows like Clash of the Grandmas, Bridezillas, He Shed---She Shed, Ice Road Truckers and Catfish, it just goes to show you how the networks can make a show out of ANY SITUATION. Real life IS stranger---and often sillier---than fiction. There's even one called Mental Floss, a brain-teaser show. REALLY?

U

Ugly Christmas Sweaters

You just have to jingle after you see these. They're so ugly, they're cute. Kind of like bulldogs. Marketing people have capitalized on it, and you can find a host of ugly sweater websites where you can buy a ready-made creation. The uglier it is, the more expensive. Or make one for yourself with one of dozens of "kits" available. So you can get additional wearage the other eleven months of the year, cut off the sleeves and wear it to one of those "Christmas in July" sales. Who knows, they might give you a better discount for your effort.

Undercover

Do some undercover "jingle." Visit the actual facilities and/or attend events of local charities that appeal to you. Like the TV show, *Undercover Boss,* you could be some lucky non-profit's Undercover BLESSING. Find out who they are, what they need to accomplish their goals, and make a donation to a charity of your choice...and at the time they need it most. It can be your time, a cash donation, medical supplies or equipment for an inner city hospital, toys for a daycare center, or new instruments for a struggling music program at a local school.

V

Vacation

People can't wait to go on vacation every year. And the media starts their seasonal bombardment early in January to be sure you know about those getaway "opportunities." It can be a lot of jingle, but you also need to think about what you want to accomplish. You want to "get away from it all," but you pack 6 bags of "it" and take it with you. You want a break from friends and family, but you wind up spending a third of your time sending postcards and texts to those same people telling them "Wish you were here!" You try to get a full year's worth of jingle into those two or three weeks a year, when instead you could take a "stay-cation" and RE-ALLY relax. You don't have to go to work! Just hang the hammock in your backyard. Most people I know spend the week AFTER vacation recovering FROM vacation.

(And, your pets you boarded away from their own beds will be mad at you for at LEAST that long.)

Just think about the costs of hotels, too. Some of them are so expensive that I heard one guy at the front desk of a major chain ask if he could split a one-NIGHT deposit for a SEVEN NIGHT anniversary getaway for later in the year over THREE credit cards.

And make it clear when you MAKE your reservations, whether you want kid-friendly or kid-free. Nothing says awkward like showing up at an adults-only resort---with clothing optional beaches---with your two teenagers in raging puberty and a pre-teen with a LOT of questions...because you couldn't read the resort description.

But hey, if you can get away, Bon Voyage!!

Vent

I call it "vent-ELATION." You know, that relief you get when you've been able to unload your frustrations about your work, your spouse, friend, family member or life in general...to someone you trust. It's healthy for your jingle factor. It may not be as healthy for THEIRS, however, if you call, Facebook or email them for hours or days at a time. You may receive a bill in the mail (or email) for your efforts. And do remember to be there for THEM when THEY have a "bent to vent" to YOU about THEIR stuff.

Ventriloquist

My personal favorite is Jeff Dunham, but there are plenty of talented people out there. Watching one person have conversations with multiple characters made out of wood with distinct personalities and moving parts is no less than a miracle. And think about it: if you are a ventriloquist, you can blame anything inappropriate you say on who is sitting next to you!

Veterans

Give these selfless, dedicated members of our armed forces, whether active or retired, all the jingle you can. While many of them no longer bear arms, thousands still bear the physical and emotional scars from defending our freedom and our way of life. They didn't fight because they hated what was in front of them, but because they loved what was behind them.

Volunteer

Give of your time at your church, school, hospital or any community charity that helps others in need. You'll get back a lot more than you give.

Walk

Tired of your treadmill? Sick of your stairmaster? Take a walk! It's the most versatile sport there is! You can go solo, with your pet, or with someone special. Remember, life is a walk in the park. So pick your favorite and get some jingle! Walking is good for your health, helps you clear your head and take a break from everyday life. When the weather's bad, walk around the mall. (However, this can create serious stress for your wallet and cause an unhealthy drop in your bank balance.)

Walmart

Are you wondering why I included Walmart? It's a 24-hour "jingle-thon" entertainment opportunity you can attend seven days a week. It's the shopping mecca for mainstream America. It's the only place you can go where you can get a manicure, oil change, hoagie sandwich, garden tools, and watch a real-life episode of "What Not to Wear", all in one place. Oh, yes, and of course, food.

Yes, if you want to walk on the wild (and wacky) side, just stop in, find a bench near the doors, and just watch people. And the show REALLY gets good after 11:00 p.m. Here's my own Top wildest outfits and excuses for them I've really seen:

1. Woman in white PJ pants covered with bright red lip prints, accessorized by a business suit jacket thrown over a black sequined cami. She obviously forgot where she was going...or where she had been.

2. Large man in low-rise jeans. Too low. Any lower and they would qualify for denim hip waders.

3. A very tall lady in very short shorts. WITH ruffles.

4. Costumed Superman, who looked more like Yoda in tights. He could not have leapt over a tall CURB in MULTIPLE bounds.

5. Young man in grey sweat pants and hoodie, who obviously felt that his pants were merely an accessory to

the red and yellow striped boxers protruding a foot above his waistband.

6. Woman walking a man dressed in full Easter Bunny costume ON A LEASH got in trouble for parking in a handicapped zone, and told security she qualified because she had a "service bunny."

And just getting around in these stores CAN be a jingle instead of a job if you do it right. After all, these stores are so big, they need their own post office. Can't find an item you want? No problem. Grab the nearest house phone and shout "Alien invasion on Aisle 5," and you'll get someone there faster than free food disappears in the office break room. They may escort you out of the store just as fast, but, hey, it might be worth it.

Weather

A great forecast for high jingle accumulations is any day you can get outside. Everyone loves a sunny day, so bask in every one you can. Pick restaurants with outdoor seating. Sip your morning coffee on the patio. Stand outside a little longer and visit with your neighbors. However, the only blizzards I ever want to see are the ones I can order at Dairy Queen. Just saying.

I actually like an occasional rainy or cold day; I get caught up on all my laundry and housecleaning, because I can't escape the house to do anything else.

Wedding

Now, don't CRASH the bash; just attend ones to which you have actually been INVITED. I wish I had an "E"-motion" detector I could take to the many ceremonies I've attended; it would beep off the charts. It's one of the few events where you can see sobbing people who are actually HAPPY. Jingle in the hope and happiness you wish for someone else's future.

One of the funniest moments I ever saw (and this really happened), upon being asked by the officiating minister if he should begin the ceremony, an obviously irritated family member held up his hand and stated, "Well, since we haven't had a reprieve from the governor, go ahead."

Another memorable moment was voiced by the bride herself while taking her vows. Upon being asked if she would take her new husband for better or for worse, she immediately stopped the officiant after the word "worse," and said, "in spite of his driving record, train snoring and smelly man cave?"

But, remember, no matter what the experience, there's always CAKE!

My father remarried a second time several years after my mother's passing. They only wanted a private ceremony in my hometown, and were taking a trip to Hawaii for the honeymoon. But their FLIGHT had to leave from Tulsa. Sooo...I had an idea, and called my soon-to-be stepmother's family. One of the ladies who worked with me was a member of the Sweet Adelines, an international women's singing group headquartered here in Tulsa. I asked her if we could hire some of them to come to the airport and sing to my dad and his bride before they left. Keep in mind that this was a time you could actually take people who weren't flying into the terminal WITH you. She said yes, so I got on the phone. First, to my favorite radio station to schedule a dedication of a Celine Dion song to air at 11:00 a.m. with a message from the DJ, then the private car company who was bringing them here to set the radio dial so they would hear the song on their way here, then to the photographer and singers as to when to arrive, and to Parties Are Us to order the balloons (that you can never have now).

Well, for starters, the song didn't air at 11:00 a.m., it aired closer to 11:15. The DJ got caught in the bathroom. The cab driver was frantically trying to stall my dad and his wife to stay in the car until he could hear the strains of the song begin. (Dad said later he was sure that status was about to change from "fares" to "hostages" when the driver wouldn't open the doors.) Finally, the song comes across the air. They were happy, but were still thinking that was all there was.

But that was just the beginning. The family and I got there 30 minutes early with our entourage of ten ladies in red dresses, one photographer, two dozen balloons, a florist carrying Hawaiian leis, and an ever-growing following of rubberneckers. We had to hide behind the columns on the far side of the gate where they would be checking in. (Today security would have nailed us for suspicious behavior.) They checked in, sat down, and then we all walked up to them, hugged them with their leis, and introduced the Sweet Adelines. Dressed in bright red dresses fresh from a Valentine's Day performance, they sang five classic romantic songs. The pilots even came off the plane to see this event.

I have a full photo album from the whole happening I treasure (see **Keepsake**) and love to browse through whenever I think of my dad. The jingle factor was beyond amazing that day. I found out later that my dad had called my work right after the wedding in Bartlesville to say goodbye, and was told (per my instruction, because I figured that would happen) that I had to go to my daughter's school to drop off some books. He was so disappointed. Good thing that feeling didn't have to last very long...like about an hour. We threw them a reception at my house upon their return.

Weight

We all want The WEIGHT to be over. No matter how we look, we THINK we need to shed a few pounds...SOMEWHERE. Jingle no matter what size you are; God never intended us to all be the same. It's the size of our HEARTS that truly matters. So WEIGHT no more. However, I discovered the cause of my problem. I've been using the wrong SHAMPOO all these years. I mean, the bottle says, "FOR EXTRA WEIGHT AND VOLUME." No Wonder! I just switched to Dawn, which "DISSOLVES FAT". I also discovered a great way to burn 2,000 calories; just leave the frozen pizza in the oven an extra ten minutes.

I do have a post-holiday poem I wrote and read to my-self every January, HOPING it will head me off from all the holiday food for the NEXT Christmas. (hasn't worked yet).

'Twas the month after Christmas,
and all through my home,
There was nothing to fit me,
no matter where I'd roam;
The cakes I had nibbled,
the eggnog I'd taste,
At all the holiday parties…
had gone to my waist.
When I stepped on the scales,
there arose a really big number!
When I went into the store
(not a walk, but a lumber),
I would remember great meals,
no calories had been spared,
In the gravies and sauces
and pies I'd prepared.
If only I'd ignored the cookies,
the bread and the cheese,
and had the courage to say,
No, thank you…PLEASE!
I wouldn't now be wearing
my husband's old shirt,
because I couldn't pull on
MY sweater or skirt.

Wine

There are more jokes out there about wine than any other single adult beverage. So whether you're commiserating or celebrating, always, always, partake of this type of "liquid jingle" in moderation, or the next day you will surely experience the "wrath of grapes" if you don't. But there are some days that just RATE "rise and wine." A friend of mine drinks the first glass for the health benefits, and anything beyond that she gives credit to for her witty verbal comebacks and amazing dance moves. If you've had a really bad day, sometimes having those "grape expectations" for later can make it better! I mean, sometimes, Wine Not?

I was visiting my neighborhood wine shop, and was sharing with the clerk my recent bout with allergies, and the unsuccessful cures I had tried. The lady behind me said, "You're HOLDING your cure. Didn't you know that wine is a natural antihistamine? You'll get better and get HAPPIER at the same time!" And it turned out this lady was a DOCTOR! I transferred my records the following Monday.

Another great thing about wine: It goes with everything you wear!

X

Xylophone

Hard to find one of these anymore, but some orchestras still have one. It sounds like a play piano being hit with a whole bunch of little men holding hammers.

Xerox

Yes, there's even some jingle opportunity at the Xerox machine. Just look around, and you'll see copies of what people are WILLING to copy, and then FORGET to pick up on their way back to their offices. One woman left a copy of a family member's will on top of the copier, along with a her letter laying claim to the assets because she was the deceased's third cousin, and who after all had lent him her car **once** 35 years ago for 30 minutes. Where there's a will, there's a relative.

X-Box

Only for the younger crowd. I still don't know what the appeal is, but it gives some people jingle.

Y

Yellowstone Park

If the only thing you know about Yellowstone Park is that it's the home of Yogi Bear and Boo-Boo, you haven't lived. Take this adventure at least once in your lifetime. And if you're concerned you'll be traveling in an uncivilized wilderness, no worries. You can stay in everything from a Hilton to a hostel, from a Radisson to an RV park. Satisfy your wanderlust and still have indoor plumbing and take-out pizza.

Z

Zoo

Walk on the wild side...visit your local zoo. It's like having Animal Planet in your own backyard. So quit Lion around. Go get your seal of approval. Find some Monkey business to get into. The zoo is the only place you can go on a real African safari without the jungle! OR the need for AK-47s, insect repellent or mosquito netting. Animals are more like people than you might think. **In fact,** a lot of animals are nicer than some people I know. You might learn something from watching how they share and care for their family and other zoo-mates. And if you don't feel like going to the animal zoo, just visit the mall. It's its OWN type of zoo. You will definitely be in a jungle there! It's Wild Kingdom on two feet, where people will KILL for bargains!

ZUMBA

It's on TV. It's crazy. And everyone is doing it. Zumba, it's a cross between dance and Yoga. It's not because it's really zum-zum.

Zebra

I don't know, just because it's funny, I guess. And it's always the answer to what's black and white and RED all over: a sunburned zebra. Either that, or they are donkeys who are doing time for something! And they're cute, too.

About the Author

Born in Bartlesville, Oklahoma, Rita (Ray) Brumm has been writing since the age of seven, when she started penning collections of poetry to share with family and friends. She wrote each poem by hand on her Big Chief school pad paper, and "bound" her literary creations with staples and scotch tape. Her lace-trimmed, cardboard book "covers" were decorated in crayon flower bouquets. Rita's fascination with the written word and its impact on human behavior grew as she started seeing and hearing TV and radio commercials, deciding that she could "sell stuff better."

And a future advertising executive was born.

Rita attended the University of Tulsa, attaining degrees in both English and Marketing. She worked in the banking and insurance industries before starting her career in radio media, which spanned nearly twenty years.

She opened Ad Genie of Tulsa, a full service advertising agency, in 2010, and has been helping her clients enjoy the "sweet spell" of success ever since. The creative aspect of her work is what "jingles" her bell the most. While she loves any type of writing, composing humorous advertising messages is her favorite. "Because it's fun, it's engaging, and---very important----it gets results for the customer!" according to Rita.

Rita has also served on a number of non-profit boards in the Tulsa area, and has been an active member of numerous community organizations, including the United Way, Rotary Club, Asbury Chancel Choir, Bixby Chamber of Commerce, Okie Dokie Cocker Rescue, Animal Rescue Foundation, Soldier's Wish and others.

When she's not working, Rita gets HER "jingle" by spending time with family and friends, playing the piano, singing, dancing, collecting radio memorabilia, volunteering with her favorite charities, and, well, shopping!! She and her husband Bob enjoy traveling to the Caribbean, get-togethers with friends, and spending quiet time at their home in Broken Arrow.